# NONE
# OF THIS
# ROCKS

## A Memoir

## JOE TROHMAN

*New York*

Hachette Books
Hachette Book Group
1290 Avenue of the Americas
New York, NY 10104
HachetteBooks.com
Twitter.com/HachetteBooks
Instagram.com/HachetteBooks

First Edition: September 2022

Published by Hachette Books, an imprint of Perseus Books, LLC,
a subsidiary of Hachette Book Group, Inc. The Hachette Books name and logo is a trademark of the Hachette Book Group.

The Hachette Speakers Bureau provides a wide range of authors for speaking events.
To find out more, go to www.hachettespeakersbureau.com or call (866) 376-6591.

The publisher is not responsible for websites (or their content) that are not owned by the publisher.

Library of Congress Cataloging-in-Publication Data has been applied for.

ISBNs: 9780306847356 (hardcover), 9780306847332 (ebook), 9780306831362 (B&N Black Friday signed edition), 9780306831355 (B&N.com signed edition), 9780306831348 (signed edition)

Printed in the United States of America

LSC-C

Printing 1, 2022

*To my wife and kids—thank you for everything*

# Contents

# Bygone Baby Bygone

I have one distinct memory from when I was two years old. It was the summer of 1986, and the humidity in South Florida was between one hundred and two hundred billion percent. So my parents decided this was the optimum climate in which to venture to Walt Disney World with a young child. It was a mere three-hour drive from Hollywood, Florida (unfortunately), to Orlando. I imagine that the circulating air within the two-door Volkswagen Rabbit wasn't very conditioned, probably akin to what your run-of-the-mill jalopy would dispassionately waft toward your sopping forehead while your armpits fused together with muck sweat. And now here you are, a mere babe, wondering to yourself, on the verge of sobbing, "Are these tears? Or are my eyes *actually* perspiring?"

And of course, everything was very, very Florida, which is not just a state or a state of mind. It's also a term we ex-Floridians and non-Floridians alike use to refer to things that are unpleasant. And thus I likely arrived at "the Most Magical Place on Earth" a tiny, angry, wet, droopy piece of baby shit. We've yet to get to the actual memory, so I'm only basing this off my now vast knowledge of toddlers and their relationships to long, hot car rides. With two of my own in the bag, I consider myself an expert. And I don't mean that my kids are in some sort of murder bag; it's a figure of speech, man. Please, put down the phone. Do not call Child Protective Services!

Now, if you don't have a toddler, first off, congratulations! Because, under all that adorable baby fat, behind their price-less mispronunciations such as "rest or not" instead of "restaurant," lie authentic terrors: screaming, writhing, imp-like tormentors from the depths of hell. I have wondered, at times, if Satan had fucked my wife because my toddlers were ready and willing to bite and kick at the drop of one of their chocolate-covered bananas—which always was their fault. And I'm a giant wuss, so I would respond with stuff like, "Ow, that hurts!" and "C'mon, stop it!" And sure, at the peak of my frustration, I contemplated things like depositing them at the city dump. But do not fear, citizens of Earth! They are very much alive and well. *Put down that phone!*

Before I move on, I want to make it crystal clear that I adore my children; they're two halves of my whole heart, unequivocally. Or maybe I have an enlarged heart? Either way, I'd lay down my life for them without so much as a thought. But when they were still merely wobbling, meaty powder kegs of intermittent rage, they scared me. And I pre-ferred not to drive with them for more than an hour, fearing that they might jump out of their car seats, grab my head, and twist it to the side to expose my neck so they could sink their vampiric teeth into my flesh. From there, I conceptual-ize that either child would suck the life from me as I lost control of the car and drove off a cliff. Then we would cut to a wide, scenic shot of a coastal California cliffside as the car careened to its fiery destruction—*boom!* In this scenario, I'm dead, but of course the children survive, their bat wings ex-panding full width as they fly off-screen, satiated, shrieking with pure joy.

So it seems my parents were braver than I am, or maybe just oblivious. Their decision to make the multihour trek in a ramshackle, two-door banger harboring a bloodthirsty toddler, was this a feat worth commendation? I mean, the intention *was* to deliver, unto me, pure delight. But my instinct is to shake my head in retroactive admonishment, as this sounds like an objectively horrible plan. However, I will admit this was a different time: a time when people did things wantonly without considering the consequences. We had no YouTube to let us know if something wasn't worth our while. We had no iPads to quell the vicious cries of our sweltering children. This was the '80s—we went on unnecessarily long car rides, with optimistic hopes and dreams in tow, only to arrive at our destinations miserable, deflated, and hangry. For reference, I recommend any of *National Lampoon's Vacation* documentaries. Terrifying stuff.

Anyway, after three "tropical" hours, we arrived at the place "where dreams come true," and I was immediately bodily harnessed to a leash. If my gosh darn dead mother did not decide to throw out my baby photos, I would've happily included a picture of this incident. Alas! Anyway, from there my dad decided that the next "best" move was to take me on the now-defunct *20,000 Leagues Under the Sea*: Submarine Voyage ride. After extensive research (i.e., my five minutes of Googling), I discovered that the ride closed in 1994 due to flooding and has now been repurposed as the Seven Dwarfs Mine Train.

Since I don't have the ability to revisit the ride as an adult and see what all the scuttlebutt was about, allow me to lay out my first-ever memory, that of the *20,000 Leagues Under the Sea*: Submarine Voyage atrocity: picture a small, overwrought me (think Shrek but a baby), with tears cascading down my bright-red face, running in an infinity loop as our faux submarine passed by a crimson mechanical crab, its pincers raised high above its body. It was as if the crab were doing a performative, empty impersonation of a crab who just couldn't find the inspiration to crab the way Disney wanted him to crab. And this crab, he was *clearly* over it.

The robo-crab may have been the source of my dismay, but he'd had it up to *here* (above his head) with crabbing. Dare I say this robot was in a . . . crabby mood? No, let's not reduce the guy to his species. He was pissed, ready to annihilate *every* slack-jawed, mouse-capped moron peering out of their puny prefab portholes. Thinking about this today, from my current perspective as a severe depressive with a sense of emotional awareness, I really feel for that old bionic crustacean.

But at two, I had yet to tap into my clinical despair. Maybe, prior to that moment, I was happy? I *have* been told I was a perceptive kid. I mean, I couldn't see dead people or tell you the weight of a human head, but I *could* see angry people, and angry crabs—so I was emotionally in tune. And I'd like to believe that, in some form, not only was I reacting *to* the mechanical crab but I was also reacting *for* the crab, helping it to express its personal vexation and displeasure with its preordained lot. Nothing against Disney (*huge* fan, thanks for passing on all my TV pitches, by the way), but once you're locked in with them, you're locked in, and they don't give you a lot of wiggle room to be yourself. Sure, it was probably a great gig on paper, but being shackled to that gargantuan brand, it was probably killing the crab's tiny-shelled soul. Even at two, I could feel its torment. So, running in an epicycle of horror, I emoted *for* the crab, catching momentary glimpses of his ready-to-fuck-'em-all-up sentiment, contrasted against my darkly mustached, defeated father, sitting at the back of the submarine, eyes glazed with morning exhaustion.

Throughout my life, my dad has been my faithful caretaker and emotional safety net. But at that moment, he took no action whatsoever. He just sat there, looked past me, zoning out, searching for some center within the chaos. But I don't blame him for his inaction; I've now been there. Because admitting defeat to a toddler is what a wise man would, and should, do. And so my dad did the right thing, to let me spin around in my own madness until I most likely conked out in a pool of my own drool, sweat, and piss. While writing this, I called my dad to confirm everything. He said I had most of this correct, aside from the ending: he carried me out of the pseudo-sub as I screamed and kicked him in the chest.

Not long after that nautical adventure, back in Hollywood (again, the Florida one, not the Tinselly Town one), I cracked my head open bouncing underneath a metal table. I don't have a memory of this, just a scar on the back of my scalp and the many times my mom relished reminding me of this incident, *her* evidence of *my* clumsiness. To my mom, this incident was always my fault. Sure, I suppose an underdeveloped, diapered chunklet without the ability to judge *anything*, let alone sharp from not sharp, should have judged his surroundings better. My mom told me this injury occurred due to my lack of peripheral vision—something I believed to be true well into adulthood. I once told an optometrist that "fact," and she looked at me as if I had just arrived on planet Earth. To be clear, I literally believed I had some sort of medical condition stopping me from accessing my peripheral vision. Slow on the uptake, as I tend to be, it took me far too long to realize Mom was calling me a klutz. Maybe I am (I do bump into a lot of stuff), but reflecting upon this insult, I think this was just my mom's way of absconding from having to come to terms with her own shortcomings—her inability to keep an eye on her own baby and an unwillingness to take responsibility for any and all neglect.

Around this point, the point in time when the point of the metal table pointed itself into my head, Mom was less than a decade away from forfeiting a promising career in medicine due to her own medical malady—an immense, benign brain tumor that had to be removed. Lucky to be alive after the procedure, but forever resentful of what "had been done to her" (residual brain damage from the radiation procedure), Mom had issues. I can only posit what it must have been like for my mom, still in the midst of mourning her life's calling. Come to think of it, I don't think she ever stopped mourning. I don't know how I would handle having to give up my dreams and desires due to my body's self-sabotage. I don't know how I would handle the inability to think, to use my mind and all of its comprehensive and cognitive functions. I can't begin to fathom how one comes to terms with a newly mangled think box. There's a paradoxical element to this, trying to wrap one's head around the fact that one's head can't wrap one's head around *anything* anymore. And on top of all of this heaviness, my mom had this young child to take care of, day in, day out. It's complicated.

Considering the facts, I wonder if it was easier for Mom to view me as what "had been done to her." The more obvious causes of her pain were either obfuscated by skin and bone or just plainly abstract. But I was physically there, smashing my head open, doing what toddlers do best—keeping things nice and exciting when all you want to do is catch a breath.

Even though my dad ended up fulfilling dual parenting roles throughout my childhood, becoming both the loving, doting mother and the providing, protective father, he was unable to be as present early on in our embryonic family as he wanted to be. Dad was still a fresh-faced physician, working fifteen hours a day in the ER at Memorial Hospital, grinding toward a career in cardiology.

So that left Mom and me with a lot of time to "bond." And on one such bonding occasion, we went on an evening stroll from our sun-worn condominium building, set within a middle-class neighborhood, and came upon a park. On that particular evening, in the midst of that park, there stood a colossal, lit-up Star of David. My mom described it as the size of a Ferris wheel. And being a sucker for anything and everything Jewishy, she was instantly drawn to this beacon, a moth to the flame.

Seeing this humongous Star as a big fat welcome mat, Mom dragged us right to this ruling illumination, and upon reaching the destination, we witnessed a good hundred or so Jews dancing the hora around the Star—a tremendous circle of bodies, linked arm in arm in celebration. And I suppose it looked like a blast, because my mom desperately wanted us to join in the party.

Now, if I had been walking with either of my children and come upon a group of one hundred people dancing in a circle, my ingrained response would be to steer clear of these one hundred dancing strangers. This is partially because I hate dancing and am not super into strangers but also because it just seems unsafe to push your small children toward an army of gyrating adults. But my mom's intuition was the polar opposite; without a moment's thought, she tried to jump us in. However, like an entrance to a haute club, only one of us was allowed in, and the other was bounced. And thus, the strong tide of bodies, this oceanic hora, sucked my tiny torso into the wave of humans as my mother was left ashore. You see, what she failed to notice, which is mind-blowing, is that these were not just regular Jews; these were Hasidic Jews—wearing black suits, sporting large black hats, donning long beards and curly Payot with tallit over their shoulders. Oh, and all these Hasids, they were men—no women in this festive circle.

Now, if you're not Jewish and are unaware of Hasidic culture, Hasids are part of an *extremely* conservative sect of Judaism who adhere to strict guidelines about gender mixing—the men and women are not allowed to fraternize, at least not before marriage. But even then, the men won't look at most women in the eyes *or* talk to them. Case in point, I once rented an apartment in Crown Heights, Brooklyn, around 2010, from a Hasidic man named Moshe. While closing the lease, Moshe wouldn't even look in my shiksa wife's direction, and any questions she asked him, he would deliver his answers back to me, fully ignoring her existence. This obviously made her feel small and insignificant. But my wife did not grow up aware of Hasidic culture, and so she was not fully prepared for what I knew was going to be a horribly reductive interaction.

I wonder how my mom felt when a hundred Hasidic men more or less stole her son from her arms. Did she feel foolish? Because we Jews, we're raised with an understanding when it comes to the wide-ranging elements of Jewish culture, including Hasids. Either my mom had temporary blindness, unable to see the obviously Orthodox ritual directly in front of her, or her judgment was as impaired as it ever was.

Imagine losing your two-year-old child to a sea of strange men. You'd freak the fuck out and call the police, right? Well, not my mom. She waited for the dance to be done and for me to find her. And about an hour or so later, I toddled back to my mom, physically unscathed, ready for the next careless misadventure.

Being the young, hot cardiologist on the scene, my dad was ready to burst out of the seams of his Memorial Hospital pants and hop into a newer, bigger pair of doctor pants (i.e., apply to a new hospital, not get larger scrubs). And speaking of bursting seams, my mom was getting too big for her own britches, growing quite pregnant with my brother-to-be. On top of that, our two-bedroom chameleon terrarium of a condominium was not fitting the family-of-four paradigm my father had envisioned. And so, with Disney World horrors and oversized ethnoreligious symbols in the rearview, we left Florida, landing in another swing state, Pennsylvania—settling in bustling Philadelphia, home of that oh-so-famous creamed cheese.

We were only in Philadelphia for about two years, from 1987 to 1988. And our time spent in the City of Brotherly Love was neither miraculous nor horrible—it was just this necessary transitional moment, like a rebound relationship, not to last for more than a blip in time. We lived in a rental home next to a parkway. It was a far bigger home than what we had in Florida, but it wasn't ours. My dad was still working to the bone, nowhere close to where he strove to be as a physician. And my mom was toiling through pregnancy, something she always spoke about with vitriol. And then there was me, spending my time playing in a mud-caked backyard, listening to the supersonic zooms of constant speeding traffic.

Outside of the experiential blandness, I actually reflect upon our tenure in Philly as a weirdly positive time, as that was when I became a big brother. I can still remember my childlike fervor and the barrage of questions: "What will my new brother look like? Will he talk? Will he do Transformers with me? Will we be best friends? Will he like chocolate? AHHH!"

I was a hyperactive, social kid, deeply wanting for a friend. Or two. Or ten. My parents told me that in preschool I once got ahold of the school's phone directory and discovered how to call my classmates, on a rotary phone, asking if I could come over to play "Elmo." I don't know what this Elmo game entailed, but my dad tightly holds on to this story as truth. Regardless, whether the story is truth or an amalgamated, semicontrived memory, my desperation for companionship was real and palpable. I needed Mom to push this kid out, like, yesterday.

Becoming a brother is one of the few things I look back upon with immense fondness. I was approaching four years old, which I think is a great time to thrust a new sibling onto a young'un. A four-year-old can grasp the concept that there's a new human on the cusp of entering their life, the exciting notion of a built-in playmate. Four-year-olds also lack the understanding that, inevitability, this new person, this seemingly harmless baby, will ultimately usurp their serene, only-child existence, ushering in a new era of bickering and brawling. But until then, I had only unparalleled, expectant joy.

The morning my brother, Samuel David Trohman, was born, I was elated. I eagerly trotted in the hallway of the birthing center, playing another made-up game, Dinosaurus Rex, with my grandparents; I think the rules of the game were that I was a dinosaur. Then, from seemingly out of left field, my mom, in a wheelchair, gradually rolled toward me. This was one of the few moments in my life I can remember Mom smiling, though I now wonder if her glee had more to do with being done with the labor than with the fruits themselves. I understand, to the best of my ability, that labor is beyond painful, a pain we men could never handle. I've watched it happen. I don't want to do it. I'm very glad I *can't* do it. And I am eternally grateful to my wife, and all women, who have given us lucky dads beautiful kids.

But what I mean here, regarding my mom and her second time through the labor loop, is that I don't think her elation was tied to having a new baby. She loved us, my brother and me, just not in the way you'd expect a mother to love her kids. It certainly was never with the words "I love you," and it never involved hugging, accolades, or a great deal of emotional support. She wanted us to succeed and not die—and I think there's some love built in there . . . somewhere. So it's not that she wasn't glad to have another child, but knowing my mother, she probably was happier that she was done pushing said child out of her child hole, which . . . I guess I can't blame her.

But regardless of her feelings at the time, mine were huge and full of outward love. The metallic crib moving in tow behind my mom slowed to a halt in front of me. I vividly recollect everything: propping myself up on the crib and looking into the bassinet. Most of all, I remember Sam, tiny, shriveled, in a white hospital-issue onesie. I smiled, ear to ear. I'm smiling thinking about it right now. Few things have made such an impression on me, let alone an impression during our grayscale occupancy in "the Birthplace of America."

It wasn't until the early 2000s that another impression was made in Philadelphia—one where I more or less "impressed" Fall Out Boy's old cargo trailer into multiple parked cars while careening our van down a narrow side street. The band was en route to the now-defunct Trocadero Theatre and running *very* late for sound check. We were not at a point in our career where late looked good on us, and considering that overreacting is one of my go-to reactions, I was hauling it. I distinctly recall the narrow brick-lined street we had to pass through, the second-to-last turn before making it to the venue. This tiny throughway was sandwiched claustrophobically between industrial buildings—a pathway more appropriate for a whimsical horse-drawn carriage ride, or an even more whimsical hipster-drawn fixed-gear bike rickshaw taxi.

Due to my speed, my naturally bad driving, and the bumpy terrain, the van's trailer—containing the band's most salient possessions, our instruments and merchandise—began to violently ricochet from car to car, smashing and crunching away people's hard-earned lease payments. It was as if I were role-playing as a blond-haired bully from an '80s comedy, trying to smash nerds at a county fair bumper car ride. My coup de grâce was upon our arrival at the venue, when I made one final crash into an Oldsmobile driven by a middle-aged metalhead who did not yell at me *and* who regaled me with stories about seeing Metallica perform with Cliff Burton. Furthermore, this car I hit—it was not his. It was his elderly mother's. And yes, we also did not have insurance. Assholes.

But back in the '80s, my parents did have car insurance. They still do . . . well, the living one does. Back then, they used their fancy-pants car insurance to move us, once more, to yet *another* swing state: Ohio! South Russell, to be exact. Oh, you don't know where that is? That's because *nobody* does. To find it, I have a patented never-fail method: open up your computer and look for it. You know how to Google shit. Don't put that on me, dick! Just kidding; don't Google it. It doesn't matter.

This move was my dad's big break, so to speak. He landed a job in cardiology at the prestigious Cleveland Clinic and used the earnings from this new position to buy our first home. While it would've behooved him to buy something closer to Cleveland, buying something an hour away from the city afforded us a big, however cookie-cutter, dwelling. We went from a seven-hundred-square-foot rental in Philly to a three-thousand-square-foot vinyl-sided traditional all-American McMansion, sitting on three-quarters of an acre of land. All that hard work, all that persevering my dad did, it paid off.

People often say that while one shoe may stay firmly affixed to a proverbial foot, we often end up waiting, with bated breath, for the other shoe to drop from the *other* proverbial foot. This is when everything good goes *not* good. So the moment *that* shoe drops, normally with a *thud* or *thud*-like report, we know trouble's a-comin'. And that other shoe, the dropping shoe, our family's dropping shoe, well, it came in the form of the move to South Russell. Because, you see, at this point, South Russell had not known many a Jew, let alone four Jews of different sizes. And everyone from our neighbors to my classmates to the townspeople, they had strong feelings about four different-sized Jews invading their Jew-less province.

Although I never consciously considered this until right now, South Russell, Ohio, is where my personal development really began—the unpleasant yet enthralling journey toward self-discovery. I don't mean masturbating; that was years later. To quickly sum that up: I was eleven. Skinemax. Basement. Cum.

This very *non*sexual journey was the first of my many wanderings that would lead me not just to where I am today but to *who* I am today. I would learn what it was to be a Jew, in the ethnic sense, through being the *only* Jew in town and being reminded I was the *only* Jew in town—through both genuine curiosity and legitimate revulsion.

But, strangely, this is also where I discovered punk rock. Now, South Russell isn't a very punk place; it's flat and isolated, and people use the word "y'all" without being in any proximity to the Mason-Dixon Line. (Or has that been officially renamed the Florida-Georgia Line? I'm a bit behind on cartography and such. I'm also an unqualified moron, but I think it's a good idea!) Regardless, South Russell was a very lonely place. And while living there, I became a very lonely guy. And as a lonely guy, I was hopelessly searching for something to identify with, to feel less alone. I wanted to be a part of something, something larger than myself that wasn't so pre-ordained, as Judaism was. And the moment I was exposed to punk, not just as a genre of music but as a full-on culture, that's when I began to find my sense of personal identity outside of just being a Jew. But funnily enough, given my family's history of ostracism in Europe due to being Jews, punk culture felt like a familiar and a natural thing to gravitate toward. Jews and punks have both dealt with excommunication. And we take pride in our strong sense of community. But it's kind of ironic how I discovered the thing that molded me into who I am today, and that made me love myself, in a place that hated me more than I could ever hate myself: the open terrain of Northeast Ohio—the worst place I've ever lived.

# That's the Power of Hugs

Idon't care about sports. I care more about Huey Lewis and the News's third album, *Sports*, than I do about the activity of sports. I'd prefer to "walk on a thin line" rather than get walked to first base. I'd be much more inclined to take a "new drug" than I would to take one for the team. And I'd sooner go "uptown to see my cousin" who "plays his guitar," which "sounds like a chainsaw buzzin'," than sit through nine innings of leisurely baseball. But that's often what I did growing up: I sat through *a lot* of baseball. Because that's what my dad loves. And I love my dad.

The great American pastime was one of the only things my dad and his late father, my grandpa Jack (or Yank, as he was Yiddishly referred to), connected over. And when my brother, Sam, started playing Little League, my dad was thrilled, taking a great deal of interest, investing in Sam's sporty proclivities. When our family eventually moved to the suburbs of Chicago, Dad managed to finagle Sam batting lessons from ex–White Sox left fielder Carlos May. Like I said, my dad loves baseball. And he *loved* the fact that he had a son who loved it too. His pride swelled when, years later, Sam became a varsity pitcher, honing a ninety-plus-mile-per-hour fastball, eventually garnering multiple college scholarships. Meanwhile, I excelled in things like drawing Sonic the Hedgehog, not being good at skateboarding, and learning every guitar part throughout the first minute of Kansas's "Carry On Wayward Son." As a wayward son myself, I am proud to say that I've never played one organized sport in my whole life, and I have the basement body to show for it. It's "a shape."

But my dad wasn't one of those fathers who would look to his athletic son, beam with pride, then look over to his other son—the total wussbag—and throw a punch at his little wittle baby teeth. Nor would he shake his head, click his tongue, and, with a remarkable sense of shame, sigh a big, "Perhaps it's better this way," then put me out of my misery, Anton Chigurh style—one clean cattle gunshot to the head. And no, afterward he and my brother *would not* walk into the sunset, arms draped around each other, my dad lovingly articulating, "I'm so glad that stupid little bitch is dead so we can love sports like men do."

My dad is awesome. And despite the fact I never took to athletics, he took a great interest in everything I liked. He loved that I became a guitarist, because he was, and still is, a massive classic rock head, which they just called "rock" back in his day. My dad exposed me to amazing films, important comedies like *Life of Brian* and *Blazing Saddles* and bizarre dramas like *The Last Temptation of Christ* and *Full Metal Jacket*. But there was *one* sport we did enjoy together: bowling. To this day, I still love to bowl. I own my own ball: she's pink; we call her "the Lovely Lady." Not to be a sexist pig, but she is a curvaceous jaw-dropper. And since my dad did a wonderful job finding things we could also bond over, I grinned and bore through years of sluggishly boring baseball games and conversations, knowing it would make him happy. Because I love my dad.

So when I first started making some money, vis-à-vis Fall Out Boy, I wanted to get something meaningful for him, a truly thoughtful, singular gift that said, "Thanks for the decades of proper child-rearing! Solid effort all around, my good man!" But Richard "Dick" Trohman is a hard guy to buy for; he doesn't care about stuff. I don't remember him having anything that was truly his, other than his Certified Pre-owned Lexus LS 460, which was less of a possession and more of a receptacle for thousands of medical papers and ECG charts. He had them stacked so high in the back of the car, on the floor, that when you would sit in the back seat, your feet were level with the seat itself, your knees up to your head.

No, Dick does not have much of a use for worldly possessions, outside of what he needs to get through the day. His enjoyment was never derived from spending money on things but from spending time with the people he loves most. But I like to show my appreciation for people by getting them stuff. I like stuff. I collect toys, whiskey, guitars, records, receipts, socks—if it's a thing or a stuff, I probably have a collection of it. For me, emotions are tied up in tangibility. I feel a sense of elation and nostalgia in seeing the things I own. They can bring me back to a place of unmitigated joy. So buying the right gift for my loved ones is important to me. Not only do I want said gift to represent something for them, but I want to make sure I can tie a great memory to the gift. So yeah, there's a selfish element, I suppose, but it comes from a place of wanting not just the thing but the entire experience itself to feel special.

However, I had a doubly hard time buying something special for the man who doesn't care for things. I was determined to find a "stuff" that would blow him away. And so, as I dug deep into my gray matter, I thought about all the baseball gobbledygook he had spoken about over the years, and a name kept popping up: Hank Aaron. Now, I have never cared about or listened to 99 percent of the sports trivia my dad has ever uttered. You couldn't pay me enough to care. You couldn't torture me enough to care. Shove ice picks under my nails, waterboard me, put things in my stupid butt—none of it will work. Sports is not happening here. Yet I knew Hank Aaron was my dad's all-time favorite player. And I actually knew who he was, on a more global scale, as an iconic athlete who broke racial barriers. But it goes to show that while I don't care about the actual thing my dad likes, baseball, I care about my dad.

And so I went to a sports collectible shop and, with zero sports knowledge, exposed myself to feeling like the dumbest idiot in Smart Town, all so I could get my dad a baseball bat signed by Hank Aaron himself. It came with a letter of provenance too. This thing was legit, and legit expensive. I didn't care, especially after I presented the bat to my dad. I got to see a man in his fifties smile like a five-year-old. I got my dad not just a great gift but something that would send him to a happy place every time he set his eyes on it. And, selfishly, it made me feel like a good son.

Days later, after the "bat mitzvah" (not the ceremony for Jewish girls but the "mitzvah" of giving someone a bat), my parents had some subcontractors over to their house to patch things up, local guys they had known for years. They had some shitty pipes with shit leaking out of them, or something of the sort. And at one point, while my mom was directing the subs around, one of them happened to notice this gorgeous, Hank Aaron–signed baseball bat hanging on the wall of my dad's home office. So my mom, noticing this guy admiring the bat, just gave it to him. She flat-out told him, "Take it." At least, that's about as in-depth as she got when I asked, beyond flabbergasted, "What the fuck happened to the bat?" I was nearly in tears, and my mom just shrugged and said, "The guy wanted it, so I told him he could have it," then walked off, unfazed, as I stood there, trying not to fall apart—fully embroiled in a *wonderful* mixture of anger *and* dejection. In an instant, my mom did what she would often do: emotionally blindside me, much akin to whacking me upside the head with a baseball bat.

Plainly speaking, my mom was mentally ill my entire life. I don't know a version of her before the brain tumor—not the glioblastoma that killed her in 2014 but the first one, back in the 1970s, the one that led to her losing touch with reality. And what I actually know about my mother's story, leading up to the tumor, is spotty. But I do know that Catherine "Cathie" Marlene Babbin was born May 4, 1952, in Birmingham, Michigan, to a family that was far from a warm, safe place to land.

Cathie's dad, my grandfather, Fred Babbin, was a six-foot-three lawyer, a stern and stoic man who maybe said one thing to me his entire life, which I believe was, "So . . . do you go to school?" I was nine or so, so it would be safe to bet that *yes*, I went to school. Other than that interaction, I don't remember much about him, aside from that when I see anything *Addams Family* related, when Lurch is on-screen, I instantly think of Fred.

Cathie's mom was Helen Babbin, a bubbly, energized lady who would send me one handwritten letter a week, with a stale piece of chewing gum attached. I love stale gum. Apparently, Helen turned Grandmother of the Year as a way to do the whole "mom thing" over. Cathie never had nice things to say about Helen, other than that she was a lousy mother. But my mom tolerated her for the sake of my brother and me—good on her for doing so too. She tried, my mom. Cathie also had a couple of siblings, who are two different sorts of cruel. I've been more or less estranged from them for the bulk of my life.

Growing up in the Babbin household sounded like an alienating existence. While Fred and Helen had three kids, they didn't seem much interested in spending time with them. To boot, they did a fair amount of keeping up with the Joneses and overspent what they had to convey this idea that the Babbins were living the high life. And to satisfy the parents' urge to seem rich while avoiding the children, the kids spent most of their time with a hired nanny, a lovely woman, from what I have been told, but not a parent. There's just no substitute.

I've also gathered that from her early childhood, all the way through high school, my mom felt isolated in the world. She was a smart woman and, in her youth, quite beautiful; to most, that's a winning combo. Yet she was socially alienated throughout her school years, partly due to negative feelings toward Jews in the 1950s and '60s. Coupled with an ice-cold homelife, I can only imagine the pain she felt, living as an island unto herself, with little outside understanding and support. But Cathie was a strong person and found ways to persevere. She threw herself into athletics, mainly tennis and cycling, in an effort to find some escape and relief.

Near the end of her high school years, she would bike the 120-mile trek to Windsor, Canada. Anything to break free. The moment high school ended, she went international again, but this time to Africa, backpacking across the savannas, even at one point unintentionally entering the Congo and at another getting attacked by wild boars. Apparently, she would rather be in imminent danger than risk one more moment back in her dreary homelife.

Upon her arrival back in the States, Cathie excelled in undergraduate school, attended a Duke University graduate program, then ended up in Ann Arbor, Michigan, for medical school. Sure, she was proximal to her family once again, but not close enough that she had to see them much. Regardless, she was on her own, in a lively college town, and could continue to forge her own path. Cathie finally found freedom, a social life, understanding, a purpose, and her own identity— the whole kit and caboodle. She was going to be a doctor. She was going to put that big, smart brain of hers to work helping others. Who knows, maybe she'd even change the world. But of course, we can't forget the complementary accoutrement to a seemingly triumphant act one: the act two break—the tragedy.

During medical school, somewhere in her late twenties, Cathie was diagnosed with a brain tumor. It wasn't all horrible news, as the tumor was not technically deadly, just a massive lump of cancer-free cells. However, it was growing, rapidly, and a growing tumor next to a human brain does not lead to a wonderful partnership. To make matters worse, the idea of physically operating on and removing the tumor was a big no-go—doing so would cause irreparable damage, potentially death. The only way to destroy the tumor was to radiate.

Now, this was the 1970s, and radiation therapy was not what it is today. Today doctors can pinpoint specific areas to radiate, affecting only the parts of the body that need said therapy. But forty-plus years ago, doctors would just soak the whole body, head to toe, in unmitigated radiation, then move you on your merry way. If you're not entirely aware of how radiation can be harmful, see the Chernobyl disaster of 1986, which, aside from the immediate death and destruction due to the explosion, the radiation, and fallout from the blast, also exposed every person out of blast range to some form of cancer, not to mention a variety of organ dysfunctions and other severe, life-threatening illnesses.

So when my mom received her radiation therapy, not only did they hit the tumor, but they also hit the entire brain—probably more. The good news was that the treatment killed the tumor. The bad news was that it also destroyed the way my mother's brain had worked up until that point. Atop that slice of sweet misery pie, the doctors gave her about ten years to live before the effects of the radiation would come back to finish off what the tumor had started. And while she beat the physician's prognosis, by a good thirty years and change, Cathie would never be the same again.

Soon after the procedure, my mom attempted to return to medical school—determined to soldier on. However, it was no use, as Cathie's ability to concentrate and access memories had been destroyed. And no matter how hard she tried, she began to struggle academically, a first in her entire life. She couldn't continue with medical school. Her dreams of being a doctor, of distancing herself far from her emotionally cold, dismal upbringing, were falling apart in front of her eyes. This was a sick twist of fate, some real fuck-you irony—no matter how hard my mom tried to escape pain, pain was poised around the corner, ready to pounce when she least expected.

Not long after dropping out of medical school, my mom was introduced to my dad, another doctor-to-be. They quickly hit it off and soon after had little old me. Remember little old me? I'm the guy whose book you're reading!

From time to time, I try to put myself in Cathie's shoes, back in '84, shortly after I was born. Years earlier, she was traveling the choo choo train of success. Then . . . *crash*! In an instant, everything was derailed. In lieu of becoming a doctor, she became a doctor's wife. Instead of experiencing success, she experienced someone else's success from a distance. That was supposed to be hers. Had my mom ever had that thought?

Was she jealous of my dad? And then there was me, the crying newborn, a responsibility that she managed on her own while my dad was working in the ER. I imagine young Cathie—alone, exhausted, staring into the black night, the stifling Floridian summer heat working up a mean layer of brow sweat, a baby howling in the background—wondering what she ever did to deserve this.

In my teens, my mom would utter here and there, out of the blue, "I hate what happened to me." I knew what she meant. I understood where her anger came from. It wasn't just that the tumor, and the subsequent procedures, robbed her of a career. No. Cathie hated living with a damaged mind. She lost a lot of what she once knew but somehow didn't lose the awareness that she used to know more and could, at one point, function better. It's a cruel fate, living with a severe disability while blazingly aware of it.

Cathie was angry at the hand she had been dealt. For most of my childhood, she carried a great deal of rage, a deep river of resentment that flowed strong up until the moment tumor number two produced itself—the big, bad cancerous one that ended it all. When one carries megatons of raw, untreated emotional pain on their five-foot-two frame for decades, those explosive emotions are going to come out sideways. They're going to make sure anyone and everyone standing within the blast radius feels their pain. Yet as a desperate son, longing for a mother's love and affection, I put myself in that line of fire over and over again, only to feel her pain transferred onto me ad nauseam, eventually amassing megatons of my own pain.

As a child, when I would approach my mother for a hug, I would often be met with hands pushing me away in disgust. Logically, it made no sense, a mother rejecting her son in such a literal way. It took decades for me to understand that I had been approaching Cathie from the wrong angle—there was no logic. All logic that had once existed in her mind had been medically scorched. But as a kid, that concept was impossible to grasp. And so I continued to try to find where Cathie's emotions might be hidden, poking and prodding with what I saw as my infectious love. But she was immune.

Cathie never uttered the words "I love you" until my mid-to-late twenties. Throughout my young life, I was left wondering if my mother loved me at all. And if it weren't for the warmth I received from my dad, as a counterpoint, I'd probably be sitting in an interrogation room, being asked where the bodies are buried. The confession tape would be available to watch streaming on Hulu via Investigation Discovery's *Murderin' Mama's Boys*.

Motherly spurning would be a daily occurrence while growing up in my household. And like a moth to the flame, I couldn't help but try again and again, to see if today would be the day Mom would accept an embrace or if I'd get burned once more. And after my routine singeing, I would go to my dad for a cooldown—some consoling.

Since Cathie didn't seem to carry many of the traits one would hope for in a mother, such as maternal instincts or love, my dad was forced to fill dual roles in my life—to be a fatherly provider and motherly safe space of warmth and kindness. He is well built for affection and comes by sweetness naturally. Some of that is nature; some of that may be informed by his own childhood, which was rife with his own disparaging parental figures. Plus, I think he knew that this was what he signed up for—he knew who he married. However, in the moments where I had been so harshly rebuffed by Cathie, I wanted Dick to walk up to her and scream, "How dare you treat our son this way!" Now that I'm married, I realize that would have put my dad in a precarious position. Yes, he had to be on my side and give me what I needed, but he also had to defend his wife, who he knew was suffering from real mental illness—someone with a scarred mind, genuinely so.

Without having CT scans and MRIs in front of us, two types of scans that I'm not qualified to read whatsoever, my family and I have theorized that the radiation therapy my mom endured most likely caused damage to her limbic system, the part of the brain that regulates emotional responses. It's quite possible that, due to this, she was, in earnest, unable to show love and accept physical affection. Plus, if there was any prefrontal cortex damage, that would explain the verbal and emotional beatdowns, ones where she would poke fun at what I looked like, or the shame she would make me feel due to my wetting the bed well into third grade (again, the bodies, where are they buried?). Group that with her less than ideal upbringing, and it's no wonder that Cathie had a hard time being kind, warm, and levelheaded.

After some of the worst interactions with my mom, Dad would do his best to explain that she did love me but that verbal expressions of love and deep emotive connections were beyond her capabilities; she was ill, and for my own sake, it was best to try not to take it personally. But for a kid, none of that made *any* sense. And for a very emotional and sensitive child, whose love language was very much steeped in *love*, through verbiage and physicality, this was a nearly impossible task to take on.

When it comes to those I know and love, I like giving hugs. In fact, I force them upon my children as if my household were a dictatorship and I the Stalin of cuddles. I love saying the words "I love you." Every day I yearn to express my feelings of love and admiration to my family. It's as if I will explode if I do not, because I feel those feelings intensely. I don't just want them to know that; I *need* them to know that. I get a sense of comfort in knowing that they know they're loved. Even if it annoys the hell out of them. Fuck them. I will not stop. I am a vicious love monster. I will eat them with my crushing love jaws, and those who survive will be sweetly eviscerated by my piercing devotion talons.

It feels silly now, pushing forty with two kids of my own, to be lamenting on and on that *"Mommy never loved me!"* But my generation, the "dreaded" millennials, we seem to be quite all right with the wacky notion that since we come from our parents, our trauma does too.

So to be true to both myself and my generation, allow me to say what we are all probably feeling: Mom, you blew it. You made me feel unlovable. You made me feel more desperate to be held than I'd like to admit. When I showed you Fall Out Boy's first-ever write-up in *Rolling Stone*, complete with a photo of the band, you didn't need to say, and only say, "You look terrible in this." As much as I dig my sexy body dysmorphia, I'd prefer for you not to have given it to me. I don't enjoy thinking about the fact that you used to throw bottled condiments at my head when we'd argue or that you locked me out of the house on more than one occasion. And of course, I had to hide stuff I owned for fear that you'd decide, randomly, that today was the day to throw out my prized possessions.

I suppose I could put together a bigger litany of things done and said by my mom, getting *real* granular, but that would get tiring. While abuse, of any kind, on every level, is abhorrent, it's also exhausting and depressing to hear about. Heck, it's exhausting to write about; I'm taking power naps in between keystrokes here! So let me get to the other side of this strange hill, because while there's a lot to resent, a lot to cry over, and a lot of dead, maggoty weight to carry on my back, there's a lot I've left out. It's less that there are two sides to every story and more that people do not exist in shades of only black or white. There's a gradient spectrum here.

Relationships are complicated; that's not a groundbreaking fact. I'm honestly angry that I wrote that because it's so incredibly obvious that no one needs to ever write that down. It's like saying, "Air is very breathable," "food is for mouths," or "Have you tried shirts for your tummy?" But it's worth noting that my unhealthy, toxic, tumultuous relationship with my mother was also smattered with moments of love, shown in her own way.

My obsession with horror movies, for instance, is due to Cathie sitting me down and screening things like *The Omen*, *Poltergeist*, and *Halloween* starting at age seven. While those are incredibly inappropriate films to show a child, and thus give further insight into her warped mind, it felt like she was letting me into a cool, forbidden world just for adults. And even though treating me as an adult when I was only a child probably did more harm than good, it made me feel mature and capable of anything, in a strange way. I mean, if I could handle watching Damien's nanny commit public suicide, I could handle anything, right? It was obvious that Cathie wanted to regard me as a peer, not just someone to make snide comments and mean jokes to. There's a sweetness buried in there, somewhere, as if she had only me to share her interests with. It was the closest I'd get to a hug.

Cathie was a patron of all arts—music, visual, written. If the medium took creativity to make, she admired it. And it was her, my mom, who nurtured my love for music and visual arts. It was my mom who allowed me to go on my first tour as a newly minted teenager (again, highly inappropriate). And after Fall Out Boy broke, apparently she would tell everyone and anyone who would listen how proud she was, even if she wouldn't tell me.

In my late twenties, Cathie suddenly started to tell me she loved me. This was after two decades of never uttering the phrase "I love you." I had stopped trying, a decade or so prior, to both hug and squeeze any bits of affection out of that woman. Yet, on her own accord, she wanted to tell me she loved me now. And she started to give hugs, not tight ones, but hugs, nonetheless. I never understood what prompted her to *feel* all of a sudden. Was her brain healing? We have surmised it possible. Or was this part of the early-onset dementia, a result of the radiation therapy? Was she forgetting who she once was and becoming this new, slightly more pleasant person? Without ever being able to really know the truth, I let her do what she was doing, as it was nice for a change. I didn't need to hear "I love you" at this point; it was far too little, too late. But it made my mom feel nice, and that made me feel a little less wounded.

A few years later, Cathie got a glioblastoma. These types of tumors are quite malignant, inoperable, and come with a short-term life span—three months, in her case. It was a rough go; she rapidly declined and lost most of her ability to communicate within the first month. Month two wasn't much better, with a seemingly slower decline; I was able to visit a fair amount due to being on tour with Fall Out Boy and often coming through Chicago, where my parents lived. During one of these visits, I took her to chemo and watched her handle getting poked and prodded like a champ when they couldn't find a vein. She didn't flinch once. She was quite strong. I never realized just how strong until that moment.

A couple of weeks later, she had a brain bleed due to some of the medication she was on and became completely nonverbal and bedridden. Before she went into hospice, I flew in to be with her—I wanted to see what had happened to my mom. As her son, it felt like my duty to see her through to the end. It was only fair, it seemed, since she gave me life.

The bleed caused Cathie to have bouts of echolalia; she would yell uncontrollably, not anything intelligible or at anyone. She repeatedly exclaimed "Ahhh!" as if she was in pain, but the doctor assured me that she wasn't and that this was just reflexive. But how could we really know? Cathie's eyes were wide, alert; it looked as if she was staring right through me, screaming for help. It was incredibly frightening. I stood there, frozen, with my wife, my brother, and his wife-to-be. None of us knew what to do. And this went on and on for what felt like hours but was probably no longer than fifteen minutes.

And then, without warning, Cathie snapped out of it. No one expected that, not even the medical staff. And right away, she started talking to me, remarkably lucid. Without skipping a beat, we began insulting each other, for fun. It didn't feel mean-spirited; I felt in on the joke for once. In her later years, Mom and I had developed a strange "twin language," where instead of taking her insults to heart, I began to lob them back. Things like "fuck off" began to mean "you're the best," and "get bent, shitbird" meant "talk soon!" We both knew that this was the best way to end things, dunking on each other. She called me "an ugly dum-dum," and I called her "a big-time stupid idiot moron doo-doo face." Then I smiled and said, "I love you." She told me she loved me back. After that, we never spoke another word to each other. She passed away two weeks later.

# The Bummer Chapter

M iss Buck blew a gasket every time I asked to go pee. It was 1991, I was living in Ohio, *The Simpsons* had successfully captivated the hearts of families across America, and I, in solidarity, showed up to school each day wearing the same bright-red Bart Simpson "Radical Dude" crewneck sweatshirt. Perhaps in doing so I had placed a target on my back, or front, giving people the idea that I was a Dennis the Menace type. It also did not help my cause that, on my sweatshirt, Bart was exclaiming, "Don't have a cow, man." Because Miss Buck, my second-grade teacher, had many a cow, man, when it came to me.

Almost immediately upon our meeting, Buck disliked me, fervently. I was loud, talkative, and inquisitive, and I asked to go pee *a lot*. Every five to ten minutes. She probably thought my pee was fake pee. And that the "pee" was a ploy, a pee ploy employed so I could skip class and roam the school's barren halls, just another run-of-the-mill bad boy doing bad-boy stuff. Scrawling phallic symbols on bathroom walls. Hitting the lot to steal Miata hubcaps. Setting off roman candles in the boiler room to make things go "boom boom." But alas, I was no bad boy. I was not a radical dude. I certainly did not want anyone to have a cow, man—not on my account! No, I was more a Lisa than a Bart. An obtuse Lisa, but a Lisa nonetheless.

Years before I hit my teen bad-boy streak, I was a regular ol' good kid, the opposite of every parent's worst nightmare—I never made any trouble. Actually, my biggest fear was getting in trouble for virtually no reason whatsoever. And that fear made me have to pee. Really badly. And as a staunch rule follower with no permission from my teacher to hit the head, I was left, dick in hand (figuratively), restless, fidgeting about, in sheer terror about where the heck I was going to dump all this piss.

Fear leads to pee. Always. To this day, I walk down the street fearing I may offend someone by stepping in their path and thus get yelled at for impeding their peaceful stroll. Just *thinking* about that makes me have to pee. When I speak in a group setting, pushing forth a potentially terrible idea from within my ding-dong brain, I become mortified that I have uttered something absolutely foolish. From there, I'm so humiliated by the sound of my own stupid voice that all the air flees my lungs instantaneously. And then, after a couple of puffs on my inhaler, I race to the bathroom. I'm mere seconds away from the hot, yellow trickle of the famous Yellow River flowing down both legs of my pantaloons.

Did I also mention I'm deathly afraid to stretch in public? When I was fourteen, I was employed as a stock boy at a liquor store in Skokie, Illinois—and a *very* illegal employment it was. But don't worry, I was awful at my job and would steal booze to sell to kids at school. The liquor store still stands to this day, across the street from the cemetery where my mom's ashes are buried. Yes, we buried her ashes. It's difficult to explain. Chalk it up to "feelings."

Anyway, most of my day at the liquor store consisted of accumulating cuts all over my hands from opening cardboard wine boxes and cleaning out spit buckets from the day's prior low-budget pinot tasting. But there was a singular part of the day that I did look forward to. Every day on my break, I would walk down the block to the Vienna Beef hot dog stand and get, not a beef bite, but a chicken dish, of the fried and sand-wiched variety.

On one particularly sunny day, as I stopped at a crosswalk, waiting for the light to change, I felt my hamstrings tighten up. So I leaned against the light pole, pulled a leg behind my back, and started stretching. Ah, did it feel nice! But then, as if on cue, a redneck dad (which is incredibly rare for these parts), with his two yokel sons, tore by in a pickup truck and yelled out the window, "Where's the football field, faggot?" I could swear that one of his sons even gave a Nelson Muntz–like "Haw haw" in tow. In that moment I felt not just exposed but like a worthless loser, and my day was ruined, as were the months to follow. A Dexter Holland type may say I became a "sucker with no self-esteem."

While I apologize for quoting Offspring, I promise the ref-erence hurts me more than it hurts you. It all hurts. So nowa-days, stretching in front of anyone at the gym, in a dressing room before a Fall Out Boy gig, or even at my house in front of my own children makes me *so* nervous that . . . oh my God . . . here comes the pee!

I'm even quite concerned that my nasally, loud midwestern voice, coupled with my nasally, loud midwestern presence, might be a nuisance to all my friends and loved ones. On that note, I consistently bother my wife with the query, "Am I an-noying?" which really means, "Am I the most obnoxious per-son you've ever met? Please tell me no!" This puts my sweet, undeserving wife in the awkward, stressful position of having to constantly dodge and maneuver leading questions replete with intense desperation. I can tell this pushes her to the brink of insanity, placing her in a bad mood, which, in turn, kind of gets me in some sort of trouble, thus putting me in a bad mood. And I could've avoided it all by not giving in to my compulsion to know, at all times, that I am a good boy—a compulsion fueled by a profound dislike for me, myself, and I.

It's as if I crave self-anointed punishment because I think I deserve it. Looking back upon little Joe, fear and anxiety were ingrained in my persona from early on. Sure, I could blame a degree of my mental malady on my mom, since she regularly poked fun at the way I walked, talked, and looked. But I think my distress regarding getting in trouble for no good reason is not wholly a nurture thing. It's who I am, naturally speaking. Which leads me back to second grade and my naturally dreadful relationship with Miss Buck.

As laid out: I needed to pee. I had asked to pee. I was angrily rebuked. And thus, I became afraid to ask to go pee in a proper pee place, which made me have to pee more. Now, most adults in charge of childcare would have found all this piss disconcerting. As a parent myself, if any youngster under my tutelage had to endlessly urinate, I would be genuinely concerned for the child's bladder health. Maybe that's the doctor's son in me, or my hypochondria (self-diagnosed . . . hi, anxiety!), but I'd also like to think it's what we humans call that rare mineral known as empathy. But my Buck, she did not seem familiar with that concept. She did not seem familiar with being human. Nor did she seem to like children, something that should be a prerequisite for educating . . . children. But what do I know?

Regardless, Buck the Suck—just made that up—was less an educator and more a bully who targeted me due to my hypersensitivity, academic struggles, and gift of gab. I already touched briefly on this, but talking often and loudly is a trait I've exhibited since toddlerhood. I've since learned how to wield this to my advantage, talking many people *out* of buying a used car, yet in my youth I was quite unwieldy, and my many teachers and peers would use my yak-tastic abilities against me, publicly shaming me in an effort to get me to shut the fuck up. Sure, it feels bad reminiscing about that social smothering, but sometimes I hear myself talk and even my brain is like, "Dude, shut the fuck up." Even as far back as kindergarten, I was more often than not forced into a sort of time-out, made to sit facing the corner of the room as discipline for my crime of chatterboxing. I remember more about that wall than I do about anything else that year, as I counted the dried paint globules frozen in time atop the overcoated yellow-white cinder-block wall.

Speaking of yellow, you're probably on the edge of your seat wondering about all that pee, the pee Miss Buck didn't allow me to take to the appropriate urine reservoir. Well, naturally I didn't want to squirt piss into my pants. While I had already developed early-onset low self-esteem, due to some of the wonderfully negative authority figures in my life, I had yet to hit such a low that filling my trousers with liquid gold felt like the right move for me. Even dogs prefer not to soil their crates. No, I wasn't willing to let myself hit Rock Bottom: Kidz Edition.

So without putting a great deal of thought into it, I used what little ingenuity I had, approached the classroom's collective box of Kleenex, grabbed a handful of tissues, and shoved them into my underwear. From there, I emptied my bladder into the clump of processed paper, thus saturating it with wee-wee. Then, once the need was alleviated, I took the now-soaking-wet ball of piss tissues (i.e., "pissues") and dunked the agglomeration into the nearest wastebasket. And with no one the wiser, and no Bucks to give any further fucks, I continued with second grade, mostly relieved, with only a twinge of shame and just one sticky, bacteria-laden palm.

Before I go any further, I want to reassure you, my dear reader, that not only have I recovered from this nearly thirty-year-old incident but I now pee in toilets, freely and without hazard. But this strange and disheartening moment in time mirrors the many others in which I put my worth aside because I felt I had no worth to consider. Allowing others to disregard me was simple disregard for myself, a natural inclination—far easier than treating myself with care. Acquiring dignity and self-love would take time. And work. And effort. Sticking up for myself, making a case for *moi*, never entered my lexicon until I received a diagnosis of major clinical depression.

My parents introduced me to therapy at age eleven. Spoiler alert: by this time, we had moved to Winnetka, Illinois. Once a week I would get driven from Winnetka to see a psychiatrist in Highland Park, Illinois. Around the same time, I became infatuated with Judith Guest's *Ordinary People*, both the book and the major motion picture film. The story revolves around a teenager, Conrad Jarrett, who finds solace in therapy while struggling with survivor's guilt, suicidal ideations, and a cold, distant, volatile relationship with his mother. The latter was something I could *really* get into. I wouldn't go as far as to say Conrad was my "spirit animal," as he is a fake human boy, not a dead creature's ghost. But if I ever cosplay or LARP (live action role-play), I'd probably go for him over Wolverine or Gandalf, only because it feels more authentic.

But the fictional story of *Ordinary People* is set in a *real* town, that of Lake Forest, Illinois, which happens to be situated right next to the *real* town of Highland Park. So the fact that I, much like Conrad, was the son of a cold, distant, volatile mother, about to see a therapist in Highland Park, a mere stone's throw away from Lake Forest, well . . . there was this quasi romancing going on there. As unhealthy as that may sound, finding comfort and respite in misery *is* the calling card of a depressive.

I don't remember a great deal about my sessions with the therapist, though I do remember hating him and every minute I spent with him, even if he didn't deserve my hatred. To start, the appointments were scheduled at the butt crack's asshole of dawn, before school started. This meant I had to be there by seven in the morning, which meant getting up at five thirty in the morning, a surefire way to make a disgruntled, emotional, sloth-like preteen boy start his day full of fiery resentment. And then there was the therapist himself. Far from being able to fluidly talk about my problems with nearly anyone, I definitely was not ready to do the deed with a sixty-five-year-old man with *zero* idea regarding how to make a proper connection with a young kid. And by the deed, I mean talking about my feelings, not sex. Gross! You thought it, not me!

In Robert Redford's film adaptation of *Ordinary People*, Conrad Jarrett (played by a young Timothy Hutton) sees a therapist played by Judd Hirsch. I *love* Judd Hirsch. Whether he's Alex Reiger on *Taxi* or the dad in *Independence Day*, he's always portrayed this loving, warm, empathic, East Coast Jewish guy—a father figure I could easily relate to. He basically played a version of my father. But this therapist was no Judd Hirsch. He wasn't even Jewish, not that being Jewish, or male, for that matter, is any sort of deal breaker when it comes to therapy. But this was just not what I had idealized in my mind.

However, to give this doctor some credit, he was patient and tried his best to crack me without pushing too hard. Did we end up getting anywhere? Yes and no. Maybe not in his sessions, but in the long run I've stuck with therapy, and I don't ever plan on giving it up, ever. I'm a lifer. So it wasn't a total bust. Yes, perhaps he wasn't "the one," but my folks had the right idea sending me to him. I know my dad wanted to figure out why I was sullen, distant, and doing so poorly in school, considering, by all accounts, I seemed like an intelligent kid— or at least un–brain damaged. He also had to consider the fact that depressive disorders can be inherited and do exist heavily in my family.

I was diagnosed as clinically depressed at age eleven. From there I was put on antidepressant medications—selective serotonin reuptake inhibitors, colloquially referred to as SSRIs. I took them for decades and was a proud "Lexa-Bro" for many years. These meds helped me to maintain healthy levels of serotonin, a hormone that stabilizes mood and feelings of happiness. Normal people are good at making serotonin. But I, a grab bag of sad, am *very* bad at it. So I needed this help. Otherwise, I experienced symptoms such as feelings of utter worthlessness, sluggish lethargy, a crazy decrease in sex drive (or in my case, no sex? No problem!), suicidal thoughts, intense anxiety, agitation, suuuuuper *slowww* thiiiinkiiiing, and a slew of other enter-the-abyss-and-get-swallowed-up-whole-by-eternal-darkness-like-a-warm-blanket-of-pain type feelings.

I used the word "experienced" in the past tense, but not because Jimi Hendrix wants to know whether you are or not. No, it's because I have recently been taken off SSRIs and put on a series of new medications to help curb my obsessive tendencies, extreme anxiety, and uncontrollable suicidal ideations. Yeah, it's all TMI. I get it; you're annoyed. I bet you'd like it if I'd just kill myself already, but the meds are working. Sorry!

It took me well into my thirties to wrap my head around the messy, tangled web that is severe clinical depression—or as we in the biz call it, "the mopes." Over time I learned how to live with it, rather than let it consume me or, worse, try to fight the vertical battle against it. That's really the key: not to fight. I'm not saying one should submit to the dark whims of Depressor the Cruel. No. But if you have depression, and many do, you won't win a battle against it. If you can find a way to make it your friend rather than an enemy, you may find it to be a strange superpower. I heard a stand-up comedian refer to his depression as just another way to say, "I'm a realist." Regarding that, you can use depression to set expectations so low that you can never be disappointed, considering most things don't work out. It's true! Is that just my depression talking? Maybe. Maybe not.

And while keeping in mind the chemical elements of major depression (i.e., the nature), one must also account for exterior influences (i.e., the nurture). While I don't want to lay the blame on my matriarch for all my woes, it's just so easy! My self-effacing tendencies can be traced back to her harsh criticisms and extreme emotional neglect. Going back to the topic of therapy, there's this trope of the patient walking into the doctor's office, lying on a chaise longue, and the therapist requesting, "Let's start with your childhood." Nobody wants to do that. But to understand your trauma, your potential mood disorders, and/or your mental illness, you have to get at the root of the problem. And all surface problems lead back to your parents, or lack thereof.

Continuing with the theme of urine, I admitted earlier that I wet my bed well into the third grade, something that I'm regretting typing and that probably would've ended sooner if my mom had responded to the wetting with kindness and empathy. Rather, she responded with anger and a need to shame me, making a big scene out of the whole incident, or incidents. Outside of these scoldings making me feel horrible about myself, I also still have that whole "fear makes me have to pee" thing. So I'd wet my bed, get yelled at, feel lower than low, go to bed afraid that I would pee, then pee again . . . rinse and repeat. It was a veritable piss snake eating its own yellow tail.

And yeah, I know I was too old to be wetting the bed. I already typed that I regretted typing that. But let's not beat around the bush: bed wetting is for criminals. Criminals that murder. *Serial* kinds of murder. Which means . . . wait. Hold on here. Are you laughing at me? Please stop it. Right now. It's not funny, guys. C'mon, stop it. Please? Stop it! I swear to God, if you don't stop laughing this *very* instant, I'll *fucking kill you*! Oh my . . . I'm so sorry! Anyway, the point I was *trying* to make (before you heckled me, admit it) was that the maternal shame thrust upon me during my formative years shaped my sense of self, and not for the better. Not only did instances like the aforementioned ones chip away at my self-esteem, but they also led me to fret over disappointing those around me. I worry all the time about not living up to invisible expectations, and I fear verbal lashings for failure, illogically so. But hey, I don't pee in beds no more! Ya heard?

Considering I could not find motherly validation, I was driven to seek acceptance from dubious outside sources—"friends" that found me entertaining only as an emotional punching bag. During my freshman year of high school, I made such "friends" with a group of juniors. And I thought these older guys were *the* coolest. I'd venture to guess that most fourteen-year-old kids think teens who can drive are dope wizards from ultra hipsville, baby. Sorry, am I talking like an undercover cop again? Excuse me.

High school is this bizarre glimpse down a future tunnel at this idea that we're going to graduate to an exciting and fruitful adulthood. And while being an adult is not exciting, nor fruitful, I always strove toward that idea of adulthood with anxious haste. So in a deluded way, I used these "friendships" with older kids as an ill-conceived shortcut to instant maturity.

Shortcuts, also known by the truly repulsive turn of phrase "life hacks" (I just barfed), certainly have their time and place. They're great on keyboards. The best of them can help you get around five o'clock traffic. Shortcuts can even help you to be more productive in a work environment. But there is no life hack to skip human development. There's no cheat code to warp from fourteen to twenty-five. And if there were, I think the horror movie *Big* showed us just how dangerous a Zoltar can be. Side note, in that movie, a twelve-year-old has sex with a full-fledged adult woman. And even when that adult woman finds out she banged a kid, it doesn't seem to register with her that she committed statutory rape, which is still less problematic than Mark Watson in *Soul Man* but no more absurd than Ray Stantz's hot-to-trot *Ghostbusters* ghost blow job. The '80s!

Spectral suck-offs aside, I was guilty of trying to level up my age as quickly as possible by ingratiating myself with the big kids. I wanted to mature, fast. This desire may have been informed by wanting to escape the stress at home; the sooner I could grow up, the sooner I could get the hell out of Dodge. But in attempting to do so, I missed crucial developmental moments, skipping experiences I could have had with peers my own age. I ended up putting myself in situations too awkward and advanced for my nascent teen self to navigate properly. I wanted to dive into the deep end before I could swim. And by aligning myself with people outside my "age pay grade," I exposed myself to a fair amount of social failure and emotional torture.

Now, that isn't to say that spending time with people years my senior wasn't also beneficial to my growth. Most of my social experiences from ages fourteen on have been with those who were three to twenty years older than myself. And some of these relationships have yielded lasting friendships, allowing me to find an early sense of maturity that actually boosted my ego, helping me to earn the respect of people I admire. I don't think we'd have Fall Out Boy without my proclivity for aged-up friendships.

But one must keep in mind that when you're young, the developmental difference between something as slight as fourteen and seventeen is quite large. So compared to the jaded juniors that I had seemingly befriended, I was a green, naive, wet-behind-the-ears child. These juniors had already experienced things I had only read about in comics or seen in movies. They were drinking, smoking, snorting, fucking, sucking, and doing whatever else older kids do—aggressive, animalistic things that exude desperation and border on drug-addled rape fantasies.

I put a lot of my self-worth into feeling worthy enough to be spending time with the bigs. I got a natural high from sincerely believing that these legit teenagers, who I saw as world-weary pros, really wanted to be with me because they saw me as existing on the level. So it came as quite a shock when, midway through that school year, one of these juniors, a portly, pig-nosed, Buzz McCallister look-alike tragedy, informed me, without warning, "You know none of us like you, right?" I did not know this. It had never crossed my mind. This dreadful piece of news cut quick and deep. How long had I been following around these assholes like a sad, lost puppy without noticing their subtle calls for me to go suck an egg?

Needless to say, I stopped nipping at their heels. The message was loud and clear. I fucked off. I was left feeling worthless, devastated, and full of shame. The words "none of us like you" rattled around my skull the rest of the day. I already didn't like me too. And all it took was some additional confirmation that I was unlikable to send me spiraling out of control.

Later that evening I went home, took out a steak knife, and threatened to slit my wrists in front of my dad. I tried to cut the skin, but the knife was so blunt I thought I could hear it screaming, in a Jersey accent, "Hey, moron, you're killin' me over here!" The point is the knife was pointless. No skin was getting cut that day. Nevertheless, I was distraught; my despair had manifested itself vis-à-vis the worst elements of my mood disorder, raging to the surface in the form of a death wish. Truly. Not only was I embarrassed to have not known how much these guys hated me, but at that moment I hated myself. And I wanted to stop hating me. I wanted to stop feeling anything. I just wanted everything to stop. In my chemically imbalanced frenzy, suicide seemed like the best answer to a chaotic problem.

However, I didn't really want to die. In retrospect, this was a sort of performance, even if I didn't mean it to be so. I was crazed, and I felt like I wanted to die, yet I chose the dullest utensil in the kitchen, easily. Still, this was my way of screaming, "Help! I'm in clueless agony!"

Thankfully, there are few out there more sensitive to my emotional foibles than my dad. To boot, his years of working as a doctor in some of the most intense emergency rooms had prepared him for this moment, something I doubt any parent wishes to go through. Calmly, and with care, he took me to the Northwestern Hospital ER to be admitted as a suicide risk. I was given Valium, kept under observation until the evening, and then asked, plainly, if I wanted to kill myself still. I knew that if I said yes, I would be sent to a psych ward for an extended period of time. I didn't want that. And I didn't want to kill myself, at least not truly. I just wanted my pain to end. At that moment, with my dad by my side and some space to process everything, my pain felt distant—less extreme.

I went home, late that night, knowing what I had always known but had somehow forgotten: I wasn't alone. It didn't matter that those idiots didn't like me. Because I had this guy, my dad, who was way cooler and far more intelligent—he was in my corner, come hell or high water. Through this incident, I learned some self-preservation. I spent the rest of my time in high school wary of making any more school-related friends, as I found most of the other kids to be equally as vapid and self-involved as the ones I had allowed to push me to near death. Shortly after the incident, I was grateful to come upon a wonderful psychiatrist who helped me learn more about how to manage my lowest lows. He wasn't Jewish, but he was my Judd Hirsch. I learned how to become more comfortable in therapy, and through that, I honed the ability to verbally indicate how I was feeling and gained tools with which I could talk myself off the ledge, so to speak, if feelings of suicide ever emerged again.

In the aftermath of the attempt, with the help of my doctor, I started to see my illness less as a hindrance and more as a malleable instrument, something I could potentially shape and use to my advantage. Depression became a different kind of filter for me to see the world through. I stopped caring so much about the trivial social pressures that other kids valued more than life itself. I started looking toward a future outside of high school, where I could experience the real world, unencumbered by narrow civic constraints. I knew there was a place out there for me to fit into. And if I couldn't find it, I was going to Picard the shit out of it and make it so.

In a strange way, this attempt at suicide led me to look outside myself, outside my bubble. Everything happens for a reason. I read that on a bumper sticker's T-shirt somewhere. We all say or think this bland turn of phrase at some point. And it probably seems as meaningful as a big, fat "pobody's nerfect!" Yet I really do believe in the trite idiom. Not just that pobody's nerfect (because pobody nis) but also that my "bad things" needed to happen. Every terrible moment needs to happen. Because without that inciting incident I would have never ventured outside the disgustingly sterile, smug atmosphere of Chicago's North Shore and into the city, looking for like-minded people from different walks of life than my own. And I would never have ingratiated myself into the city's hardcore scene, which led to the formation of Fall Out Boy.

You know, after *all* this time, now that I've taken a step back and gotten a serious global view, one thing sticks out to me more than anything: I really need to thank that steak knife!

# May the Force
# Be with Jew

At risk of coming off as a basic bitch, I request a moment of your time to talk about *Star Wars*. And no, this will not devolve into a low-hanging "who shot first?" diatribe. Nor will this touch on the more nuanced and intellectual conversation about the best order in which to watch the series, while I seduce you with a sweet "fuck the prequels and also episodes seven through nine" in your ear. No, I want to consider why those of us who love *Star Wars* love *Star Wars*. Of course, it starts with the window dressing: the dramatic looks of the various worlds, the groundbreaking practical effects, everything and anything Jedi, the scum, the villainy, the scruffy nerf herders (you know you're one), the aliens, Lord Vader (the best and coolest movie villain of all time), the comic-relief droids, the blasters (*pew! pew!*), and a wide array of characters for everyone to relate to. Are you a wise Yoda? Perhaps you're a suave Solo. A snarky, headstrong Leia? A naive and whiny Luke? A petulant Kylo? A horny Maz Kanata?

Once you get past the gorgeous visuals and snappy dialogue, you begin to notice the Homeric poetry, some *Flash*

*Gordon*–meets–*Stagecoach* gunplay, a thick smattering of Frank Herbert thievery, and lots of Kurosawa wipes. It's no wonder that the original *Star Wars* trilogy is still so compelling: with a clear, strong vision, and theft from the greats, you have a shot at making something good, perhaps even wholly original and breathtaking. As Godard once said, "It's not where you take things from—it's where you take them to." Lucas and company took us somewhere far, far away that still makes the lot of us shit our collective pants every time the logo hits the screen and those trumpets sound off.

All the aforementioned magnetic elements of the franchise that have drawn in generations of fans are the same things that drew me in and have kept me a *Slave I* to Lucasfilm. Together we've persevered through the same general grievances, from a poorly CGI'd Jabba the Hutt, slithering around the *Millennium Falcon* like a fat man selling half-priced stereos with Sony guts out of the back of his '96 Pontiac Firebird, to Anakin sulking, "I hate sand" (don't we all?), to Jar Jar making "meesa" so mad.

But together, like a bunch of pork-ploppin' Miami Morrisons, we've broken on through to the other side. We've returned to the *Star Wars* universe with open arms, vis-à-vis the wonderful, televised stylings of Mando and Grogu, a modern-day Lone Wolf and Cub, and big boy Boba Fett, the eternal badass of bounty hunting. This Jon Favreau–led refresh has not only brought in new fans but reminded us oldies why we fell in love with it all in the first place.

Yet when I think about why *I* love *Star Wars*, why I *really* love *Star Wars*, it's less about the varnish or being able to choke people through a holographic video conference call. I was first exposed to the series in the early '90s and quickly took the whole thing personally. Yes, the aesthetics hooked me, but I fast took note of these bad guys, the Imperial Order. They were dressed like Nazis straight out of the Third Reich. And these bad Nazi guys would send out these other bad guys, stormtroopers (also a name used to refer to the Nazi paramilitary), to kill the good guys. Now, as a young Jew, I had already learned my fair share about the Holocaust. I was aware that my family history was checked with virulent antisemitic violence, especially on my father's side, from Russian-occupied Poland. And I would come to learn later in life, through forking out a fair amount of dough for a European genealogist, that I had distant relatives in the camps.

Even after my family immigrated to the US under the surname Frauman (which was Ellis Islanded to Trohman), the othering and exclusionary tactics against my family, while mostly nonviolent in nature, continued on. Growing up in different parts of suburban Detroit in the 1950s and '60s, my parents had dealt with antisemitic repulsion. Whether being told where their families could and couldn't live, my mom spending her high school years in antisemitic-driven isolation, or my dad losing friends once they discovered his ethnicity, the stigma continued, and it still does today. But we Jews soldier on. We refuse to be stomped out so easily. I mean, if pogroms and Hitler's regime couldn't kill us all, then neither will the nu haters—even if we only constitute 0.19 percent of the world's population. Close! But no cigar, Nazis!

And so back to the '90s: there I am, a young Jew, enthralled by a space saga where space Nazis get their nut sacks ripped open by a ragtag group of testicle-tearing resistance fighters and laser-sword-wielding, scrotum-slashing wizards. This was wish fulfillment at its most elevated. Watching the series made me feel faux tough during a time in my life when I was a bona fide weakling. Power by proxy!

Growing up in small-town Ohio was as Ohio as Ohio sounds. It was flat. It was milquetoast. As far as the culture went, it was predominantly home fries, white guys, and a defunct tractor production plant. The town where I went to school was, and still is, called Chagrin Falls, which roughly translates to "Sad Falls," if my grasp of English is still accurate. My time spent in Sad Falls left predominantly bad memories in my cranial sphere, because as the name suggests, it was a less-than-happy place to exist, at least for me. This semirural village is where I, along with my family, was first made to feel strange, outside, and utterly repellent.

It was the late '80s when my family moved to a lightly populated area of Ohio, about forty minutes away from the faded Rust Belt city of Cleveland. Now, if we as a family had wanted to immerse ourselves in Jewish culture and be among those like us, Mom and Dad could've chosen Shaker Heights, near the city's limits. We could've settled in Beachwood, an area that is so Jewish you can see its nose from the International Space Station sans telescope. But being among a swath of Jews, for both community and comfort, was not at the top of our priority list. We were new to town, new to the state, and my dad chose a place to reside nearest his colleagues in hopes of having a built-in social circle. Hindsight is a motherfucker: that circle never rounded out, and we became one of the most isolated families in town.

Up until that moment, when we set foot into the Wicki-Wicki-Wild Midwest, my dad, the fresh-faced cardiologist, had been moving from hospital to hospital, making a name for himself as a physician. Now a doctor at the famed

Cleveland Clinic, my dad had some of that "spendin' money" we'd heard so much about. It was wonderful at first, to have a place that was ours, a place we could finally spread out—a tract home in a quiet development with a backyard so big it was hard to determine where our space ended and our neighbors' began.

However, choosing a locale where we were culturally alien left us exposed to hyper-exclusionary Pleasantville townsfolk, donning nice outer candy shells, but with thick, rich bigotty centers. Chagrin Falls and South Russell were where I learned that no matter how much I tried to assimilate to white, Anglo-Saxon society, I would forever be on the fringes of that society. And yes, I am quite aware my skin is white, and there is the privilege that comes along with said white skin. I would never equate being Jewish in America to being Black or Brown. Being Jewish is like living in a purgatory between the "heaven" of whiteness and the "hell" of everyone else. There's this never-ending debate, which Jews are not in control of, about what Jews are: a race, an ethnicity, a religion, a mischief of rats, a global cabal. It is said that if you were to remove my skin, by unzipping me in the back, hundreds of rodents would scurry off, back to their underground bunker where they control the world's banks and churn out tired Hollywood reboots.

In late 2017, an eccentric man driving a Maserati, wearing a Maserati hat, had just T-boned my car. After I recovered from the shock and exited my fancy electric vehicle, the offending driver instantly spat in my face that I was "drunk, high, and speeding." I wasn't any of those things. In fact, due to the rain, I had been driving twenty miles per hour. He probably thought I *was* high because my airbags let off a wafting skunk-like odor. And the drunk part? Seemed like a nice thing to tack on, in his favor.

Regardless of the fact that this grade-A asshole, who fled the scene, was found at fault by the insurance company, it wasn't a great day. As I sat in the Uber, heading back to my house, whiplashed, still in shock, and stone-cold sober, I wished so badly to be drunk and high. And then the driver, a gregarious Black man, peered into the rearview. I could tell he was trying to figure me out.

"Can I ask you a question?" the driver queried.

"Shoot."

"You're a Jew? Yeah?"

"What gave it away? My face?"

Now, keep in mind, regarding the driver's next question, that we were a couple of years into Trump's presidency, a presidency bolstered by white supremacy, among other horrible tenets. Indifference toward Black lives was clear from the top down, and national tensions surrounding anti-Black brutality were making their way more and more to the forefront of the daily news cycle. It was only a year prior, in 2016, when both Philando Castile and Terence Crutcher were killed by the police, both clearly racially motivated crimes— the former caught on disturbing video. Our nation's leaders were doing little, if anything, to help ease centuries of pain heaped upon African Americans. To boot, America was at the precipice of a 24-7 sociopolitical powder keg—a never-ending cycle of horrific news documenting hate upon hate.

So with that in mind, here I am, having the rideshare of my life with this quirky, fun Black dude. I had just referenced my *Yentl* face (I can call it that!) when he dropped this bomb on me: "So what are *your* people gonna do for *our* people? Because you know that after us, they're comin' for you."

I told him we had our best men on it.

Just a few months later, at the Unite the Right rally in Char-lottesville, Virginia, neo-Nazis took to the streets to exclaim the ever-so-catchy "Jews will not replace us!"

As a kid, I just wanted to fit in. Sure, we walk into the seemingly soft and warm arms of our elementary schools with banners like "Different is magnificent!" and "It's neat to be unique!" but no one wants to be different in school. In fact, society snubs the different. We all want to assimilate, to an extent. If Jimmy has the cool shorts with the pockets and the zippers and the strings and doodads and jimjams, then everyone wants the many-pocketed jimjam string shorts. And if you don't have those shorts, you're a goddamned loser, dead to the world. I just realized I probably should've picked a better example than shorts. But I'm in too deep now to go back!

As I've grown older, I've become far more comfortable with my brand—that of a hairy, smelly layabout with Semitic features, donning a thick layer of doughnut-infused father fat evenly distributed across my abdominal region. I am proud of my physical individuality, however gag inducing I may be to others. Gag away! See how I care! And I've also been fortunate enough to find communities who understand me as both a cre-ative guy and a Jewish guy. But it's taken a long time to find my people, those who have helped to make me feel safe, sup-ported, and comfortable in being me.

But back in Ohio, when I was still an insecure little man, I was quite the outsider. As part of one of the only Jewish fami-lies in town, I was actually beyond an outsider. I was a rare creature, something to gawk at from far away or just throw rocks at and run from. No matter how hard I attempted to in-tegrate into WASP culture, I was denied left and right, reminded that a bulbous nose and head of bushy, dark curly hair were a bit too swarthy and strange for their liking.

One of my earliest memories of being made to feel othered was almost straight out of a David Cross stand-up bit, the one where he goes on about a parent of a childhood friend asking him, "Y'all's people eat oatmeal?" and then continues on to explain what this parent thinks they know about Jews: that we all "do dances in the woods" and "wear cloaks and do secret services and burn potions and whatnots." My nearly identical encounter came courtesy of our next-door neighbors. These were people so bland that I cannot remember much about them, other than they looked as if they jumped right out of a Norman Reich-well painting—blond, blue-eyed people with translucent skin who had yardsticks firmly inserted within their anal cavities for maximum straight 'n' squareness.

Right after we moved into our cookie-cutter home, among the neatly manicured lawns and community "fishin' hole," I befriended the neighbor's daughter. And one particular sunny-yet-brisk morning, the two of us spasmodically ran back and forth between our front yards as the girl's mother watched on. I can't recall exactly how the following inquiry came up, but the topic of Christmas arose, and I was asked something like, "So what do you want for Christmas?" I responded proudly, snottily, out of breath, as if it were obvious, "I'm Jewish!" and then kept running, arbitrarily.

I assumed this would quash any peskier Christ speak so I could continue to focus on aimlessly sprinting. Rather, my proclamation seemed to make the mother uncomfortable and pensive. She was now looking at me like one ogles a car wreck, with morbid curiosity. Seeing me now as an oddity, she proceeded to ask, "So then what *do* you do for Christmas? Is it something to do with sacrificing animals? To make everything 'kosher'?"

Since I was barely in kindergarten, I just said, "I dunno!" and kept spinning in circles. I started making *dubdubdub* noises. Now I was a helicopter! Man, I forgot how much I used to enjoy spinning until the point of no return—entering that sweet spot, the pre-puke zone. Nowadays, I get motion sickness just looking at someone riding the teacups at an amusement park. But back then, somewhere in my tiny mind I probably used the spew spins as a defense mechanism, an effort to mask my innate discomfort with something even more regurgitative.

My remaining years in provincial Ohio were far less "innocent." From about third grade until we moved to the Chicago area, around late sixth grade, I experienced regular terrorizing in the form of one particular bully, Eric. He enjoyed spending many of my years in Chagrin mentally tormenting me by either referring to me by various Jewish slurs—hurling the K-word was his prized bit—or reminding me, on more than one occasion, very explicitly, donning a sick grin, that he had a Nazi relative who had murdered my family during World War II. Maybe? Hard to know if that was adjacent to any truth, but he had a very German last name, one that I'd prefer to obfuscate in this text because I don't do revenge. Or lawsuits. Despite my Jewish face, I am *not* a lawyer. I'm a great guy!

When it came to Eric, if I ever tried sticking up for myself, I'd get a punch in the gut. Or if he was in an even less verbal mood, he'd sock me in the kishkes, unprompted; for reference, that's the area right below the tummy, just above the schmeckle. For a good three years, this was my daily life. And to further the mindfuckery of it all, there were times when Eric would pretend we were friends, often to manipulate me in one way or another for his own personal gain—either to embarrass me in front of peers or to score the pocket change I may have been carrying around for lunch. Classic bully!

This was my normal. The abuse and ridicule became my baseline. And while I never enjoyed the torment, I came to expect it—it became familiar. I didn't know any different, and as these were my formative years, I definitely didn't know any better. I was far too young to understand the psychological scarring this would leave behind, the way this daily torture would inform my self-esteem and my regard for my own Jewishness henceforth.

After I endured years of good-time bullying, my dad informed our family that we were to be moving from this backward shit shack to the cultural landscape known as Chicago. However, I was not thrilled; I didn't want to lose the few friends I had. (I promise to tell you about the good one soon.) Despite the daily abuse from Eric, I didn't want to lose what was familiar to me. Change is hard. So the only way to get me to change was to drag me, kicking and screaming, away from the only thing I had ever known: getting treated like a Lollapalooza porta-potty—*real* shitty.

I had reoccurring nightmares for the first week after moving to Chicago. In them, I would be walking down the hall of my former middle school in Ohio, looking at my former classmates dressed in black. They were conducting a solemn funeral procession as I frantically tried to get their attention, shaking shoulders, screaming at faces, "I'm here!" But no one would respond. They would continue on, meandering down the hallways, *om*ing like Brahmans. I wasn't there. It wasn't clear if I was dead or alive. What was clear was that I had ceased to exist.

It was also clear that this was a dream with an obvious meaning. The twist, though, came near the end, when I looked down at my pants and discovered my penis had popped out through the zipper. That's when I would finally get noticed. Everyone would then turn around to laugh, in mechanical unison, "Ha, ha, ha," while pointing at the lil guy. I would then awake covered in sweat, reminded of both my homesickness and small-dick-ness.

Moving to the suburbs of Chicago, specifically Winnetka, a town incorporated as part of the highbrow North Shore area, was quite a shock. I went from a part of the Midwest that was semirural, situated in a socioeconomic zone between lower and staunchly middle class, to a zip code that boasted some of the wealthiest in the Chicagoland area. It had a little bit of Hollywood glitz too; I could throw a stone, and it would land on a John Hughes film location. Harold Ramis lived a town over. Every Halloween, until his death, he would squeeze his portly self into his *Ghostbusters* uniform, for the kids. The drummer for one of my favorite bands, the Smashing Pumpkins, Jimmy Chamberlin, lived in the hood—it was a trip, to say the least. Oh, and there were the Jews. Right next to Winnetka, in a town called Glencoe, there was a large Jewish population and the synagogue where I was eventually bar mitzvahed.

The North Shore also includes an odd, very small, incredibly wealthy village known as Kenilworth. Upon moving to the nearby area, my parents, being the good, fearful Jews that they were, informed me that Kenilworth was not a place for us. At first, I thought it was their way of saying, "We can't afford to live there, so we're going to say that this place hates Jews." But as it turns out, they were not wrong.

Founded by Joseph Sears in 1889 on four conditions, one being "sales to Caucasians only," Kenilworth was known to exclude both Black and Jewish people from residency. For elaboration, look no further than Illinois historian Dr. Neil Gale's discovery of Kenilworth's rage-inducing signage posted

around town from many decades ago, which read, "No Nig-
gers, No Jews, No Dogs." I mean, dogs? In the words of the
great Homer Simpson, "These people were the suckiest bunch
of sucks that ever sucked."

It turns out that this disgusting signage was actually posted
in towns all over the Midwest during the '40s and '50s and was
not exclusive to Kenilworth. Yet their sentiment lingered, nevertheless. Outward hatred, like in Ohio, may not have been as
prevalent in this new homestead, but to know that no matter
how far I traveled I could never escape the painful, personal
twinge of anti-Jewish bigotry, well . . . it left me with a pit in
my stomach.

Anyway, back to Tatooine. Or as we call it in my space opera, Ohio.

# Much to My Chagrin Falls

I n case you need a reminder, *Reader's Digest* is a tiny magazine, almost more of a booklet, that exists solely to wither away in dentists' offices. It lies there, all like, "Please, read me! I'm full of interesting, semioffbeat articles!" But you don't want to read it. It's too small. It bothers you. You think you're too good for it, and it's true, you may very well think you are.

I, however, couldn't imagine having a waiting room of my own and not plastering the coffee table with *Reader's Digest* and *Miniature Donkey Talk* magazine (it's real; look it up!). To be honest, though, I've never read one issue of *Reader's Digest*; it didn't have a double-spread picture search, like *Highlights* magazine did. But my dad did press me to do their Word Power segment, very often. I mean, he didn't hold a gun to my head, but he made Word Power feel like a prerequisite to being his son.

In case you don't know about this obscure quiz within the aforementioned, wildly uninteresting, puny magazine, Word Power is basically a multiple-choice test that posits difficult, obscure words and presents you with three possibilities for what each word *could* mean. You then circle your answers, in pen if you're bold, turn to the next page for the answers, and discover you've gotten them all wrong. I only took part because

I have a strange obsession with words, and I liked doing stuff with my dad, and I wanted him to think I was a big, smart boy. So every time I'd play, I'd think, "This time I'll impress my dad, and then *I'll* be the doctor!" An example of a Word Power segment would go something like this:

*Benighted*

A) *To be knighted in the presence of a monarch*
B) *Pitiful intellectual ignorance*
C) *To prepare for a night's slumber*

The answer is B, which was my permanent state throughout my many wars waged against Word Power, and by proxy its creator, Wilfred J. Funk. Funk that guy and all, but I did end up learning a lot through being terrible at this game. Playing Word Power is how I learned that the place I was living was truly as depressing as it felt.

When I saw the word "chagrin" in a Word Power, I got really excited—that was *my* hometown, Chagrin Falls, Ohio! Well, yes, I actually lived one village over, in South Russell, but that was a place so dull that I've almost completely forgotten it existed. It's so boring that when I Googled it—like I told you not to do in the first chapter of this book—the news section only displayed one headline, "Bored Girls Climb the Walls." The implied joke is too on the nose, but the story is as real as it claims to be: apparently some teenage girls got bored, so they climbed a wall to hang out on a roof. That's the story! When I lived in South Russell, we didn't even have walls to climb, so those girls should consider themselves lucky.

Chagrin was just a short drive away and seemed livelier—it had a downtown with a locally famous Popcorn Shop, filled with a vast cornucopia of artisanal treats. I went to school there. In

Chagrin, I mean. Not in the Popcorn Shop, though that would've been delicious! Most of the people I considered my friends lived in Chagrin. It even had a river! That's where the falls fell into. South Russell just had a bunch of yellow grass and a small forest behind my house, where I once discovered a budding serial killer's secret hideout, consisting of three jars containing animal brains floating in formaldehyde, and some pornography. Holy shit, yuck, and also sort of yuck. I kept the porn.

I was drawn to where things were happening, and Chagrin seemed happening. Between the ages of six and twelve, I loved Chagrin Falls. But the funny thing is, I came to learn that that place hated me. The only reason I felt any fanfare for Chagrin was due to the fact that I didn't know anywhere else, no Chicago, no New York, not even a Pittsburgh, per se. So Chagrin Falls, Ohio, seemed like the epicenter of everything.

I used to read a lot of *Calvin and Hobbes* and was so thrilled that Bill Watterson, the creator, was also from Chagrin. On the back of one of the collected editions I had was a drawing depicting a gigantic Calvin thrashing downtown Chagrin Falls, holding the famed Popcorn Shop in the air like he's about to give it a good smashing. I thought it was just fun, until I recently picked up that same collected edition from my bookshelf and thought that maybe Calvin hated that place and wanted it destroyed. Looking back, I wish I'd had Calvin's confidence and attitude during my tenure in that town, because it would have saved me from my endless chagrin, a word and concept I came to fully understand thanks to Wilfred J. Funk, creator of *Reader's Digest* Word Power.

Let's get back to Eric, my friend who was not my friend. Eric was my first nemesis, only I didn't seem to grasp that obvious notion during the time we spent together. I was too desperate for a friendship and thought too little of myself. Eric was bigger and meaner than me and loved embarrassing me in front of his cohorts, homogenous white kids whose faces I couldn't conjure if you held a gun to my balls while poking my taint with a Buck knife. But I'll never forget Eric. He's the first person in my life who made me feel physically threatened.

For the longest time, I was desperate for social interaction. I kept this desperation up until I had my kids, which is when I lost all energy and care to socialize whatsoever.

To this day, I don't understand why Eric really wanted to spend time with me. I think, to a degree, I was a curiosity; to middle-American WASPs, Jews are these strange biblical creatures, and not many of them lived "round thar parts." Perhaps that was interesting to him. I also think I was someone Eric was fine spending time with, as long as no one was looking. I was the girl who was fun to fuck as long as your friends don't find out. And my reason for wanting to latch onto someone like Eric was simple: I had such low self-esteem I thought that, by virtue of attaching myself to someone more confident, my sense of self-worth would become elevated. I naively thought, with each new hangout, that this time he'd become my real friend and stop treating me like a piece of garbage. We also both liked Zippo lighters, a lot.

I don't know the exact reason why we both gravitated toward Zippos and their fire within. I'm sure it comes from some innately male machismo place, coupled with the fact that mastering fire was perhaps the most pivotal event in the history of humankind. Also, Zippos were shiny and expensive. Shiny, expensive, fire . . . sounds about right to a couple of dumbass boys on the town!

Most of my hangouts with Eric consisted of going to the local tobacco shop, in downtown Chagrin. The proprietor of the shop allowed us to loiter in his store, which was clearly for adults. We would stand in front of the spinning Zippo display, lusting over the lighters' shiny casings adorned with run-of-the-mill biker-dad designs—the severe bald eagle with American-flag feathers, an overly dramatic roaring lion with a flame mane, the slack-jawed Grim Reaper grasping a scythe, a Bettie Page pinup girl showing off her exposed upper back. Yowza! But I had my eye on the lighter with the peace sign, only because I was obsessed with my Woodstock '94 CD. Two more days of peace and music, baby! I made it clear to Eric that it was my dream to own that Zippo.

For eleven-year-olds, who very much looked and acted as such, purchasing a lighter, or any type of smoking device, wasn't going to happen. We didn't have the money anyway. So Eric started poking and prodding me to steal a lighter—the peace sign Zippo, specifically. He wasn't using epithets to get his way; he knew, for this scenario, he had to use deft manipulation. Eric always knew which button to press to get the reaction he desired from me. He kept telling me how cool I would be if I did this one thing for him. If I had any amount of self-respect, I would've asked Eric to rip it off himself if he wanted it so badly. But I desperately wanted his approval.

As I've explained, I was a good kid, and the idea of getting in trouble made me supremely anxious. Now here's Eric, asking me to do something that undoubtedly would get me in trouble. Maybe even arrested.

In my addled and limited mind, I had no choice; I *had* to thieve. Being cool, being wanted, that mattered more in the short term. Eric had done a phenomenal job whittling me down to the point where I felt I needed his approval to be worthy. I gave in and said I would do it, but I told Eric we would have to go to my house to get a jacket, as I was just wearing a T-shirt and had nowhere to hide the goods.

An hour or so later, we came back to the tobacco shop. It was the outset of the summer months, and I entered wearing a winter jacket. Not only was I sweating, but I also looked unbelievably sketchy—as if I was cosplaying *as* a shoplifter. Eric decided to wait outside because he was, as he would call it, a "pussy." But because I was not seeing it through pussy-tinted glasses yet, this made me ten times more nervous; I wasn't ready to go it alone. Yet he still made me feel safer just being nearby; his large, looming presence made me believe that if he wasn't beating me up, maybe he would beat someone up *for* me. Like private security, maybe Eric would punch the store's proprietor if I got caught? Unlikely, but I needed a false sense of comfort to do the deed. Up until then, my favorite pastime was watching *Terminator 2* on VHS and pretending I was John Connor. He seemed like a badass. I wanted to be badass. And Eric could be my T-800, my Uncle Bob.

So here I was, playing badass but looking like a bad asshole. As I entered the shop, the owner peered up at me from his newspaper, squinted, then looked back down. I went from sweating to pouring sweat, less from the jacket and more from nerves. And yet, even with this outpouring of water, I retained enough moisture betwixt my loins to prompt an impending feeling—an anxious piss. So with that in mind (and bladder), I walked up to the lighter display and spun it once . . . twice. I looked back at the owner, who was still reading his paper. OK, it's now or never. I looked at the display again with ultimate determination and could've sworn the peace sign lighter twinkled just for me, giving me the A-OK to become its new owner, for gratis.

I locked eyes on the Zippo and gave the display a final spin. It was illogical, but I thought if I grabbed the lighter while the display was in motion, it would somehow create a diversion—a confused idea, at best. As the display made its final rotation, the world slowed to a snail's pace; it was like a generic scene from a movie, where some guy goes to Vegas and bets it all on red as the roulette wheel spins in slo-mo. Will he win it all?

Mid-spin, the peace sign revealed itself and sparkled for me. That was my moment. I grabbed the lighter, put it in my jacket pocket, and hastily walked out of the shop, head down—a clearly guilty boy. Adding a little pizzazz to my heist, I ran into the doorframe upon exiting. I should've been caught, but the owner never looked up, not once.

Outside the tobacco shop, my adrenaline was through the roof. The rush from the theft was intense, a mixture of pure joy and utter terror. I was still in fear of getting busted. But as I briskly walked on beside Eric, hands in my pockets, gripping the lighter, we neared the end of the block, and it hit me—I did it. I really did it. I got the coveted Zippo peace sign bootleg Woodstock '94 lighter!

For the first time in my life, I felt fucking cool. I held the lighter up to inspect my beautiful bounty, relishing in my victory. Then Eric snatched it. I was confused for a moment, until I realized this lighter was never for me. While I was dejected, Eric was incredibly pleased. And I suppose I got what I really wanted out of this—to please Eric and have him treat me as a full-fledged human being for once, as if that were even possible. So this was his lighter now. And assuming I finally had Eric's approval, I allowed my dejection to turn to delight. He opened the lid to the Zippo and flicked the flint wheel. Just sparks. He flicked it again and again, but to no success. Just sparks, no flame. Eric then admonished me for not *also* stealing lighter fluid.

"It was *behind* the counter," I explained defensively.

Eric angrily stomped ahead, and I followed along like the sad, wet dog I was. After walking for miles in perpetual silence, we came upon a drugstore on the outskirts of town. Years later this place would become a CVS, but back then it was privately owned. I don't remember the name, but I remember the video rental shop next door—Star Flicks. That place had a section devoted just to distasteful movies, what the Brits called "video nasties." That's where I rented Peter Jackson's *Dead Alive* (or *Braindead*, as it's known in New Zealand) and the infamous *Faces of Death*—a disgusting wretch of a tape that I regret ever viewing. Regardless, I wish we had gone there instead. I would've rather vicariously slogged through someone else's horrible nightmare than lived out a version of my own.

Inside the drugstore was a wall of smoking products—disposable lighters, lighter fluid, a variety of cheap cigars, cartons of cigarettes, etc. This was the '90s, in the Midwest, so no one was particularly concerned about dangerous flammables and smokables being kept in safe places, away from the prying eyes and hands of children. Eric whispered to me that I *had* to get lighter fluid and a pack of Swisher Sweets cigars. "Oh my God, so we're going to smoke too?" said my inner-nerd monologue. That sounded *very* cool. And scary. But cool. Sunglasses cool. John Connor, "Hasta la vista, baby" cool.

Eric didn't tell me what would happen if I didn't commit the crime, but I didn't need to ask—I *had* to do this. I looked around, and it seemed easy enough; there were tons of other customers shopping and no employees other than those working the counter, which felt like a mile away; there was *no* way the focus could be on us. I didn't see anyone of clear authority lurking around. I had just pulled off the ultimate heist a mere hour earlier, so this would be a cakewalk. All I had to do was traverse a couple of aisles down; grab the unprotected items, which were in plain view from where I was standing; stuff them in my coat like the conspicuous dimwit I was; and guiltily shuffle out of the store, but not before running into another jamb, of course. I went from a never-done-wrong good boy to master crook within a couple of hours.

I approached the tobacco and tobacco-accessories aisle and perused. I put a hand on one thing. I grabbed another thing, removed it from the shelf, and pretended to look at the information on the back of the package. I then put it back. I was doing what I'd heard referred to as "browsing." Another first for me! I browsed and browsed and browsed some more. Browsing was stressful—especially when it was a vehicle to conceal criminal activity. Eventually I locked eyes on the lighter fluid and cigars. As my mom used to tease, I had no peripheral vision, and I believed her because it felt less like a fun tease and more like mockery of the truth. I laugh at my kids too, but *behind* their backs, and I hope they never find out (until they're old enough to read this, of course).

So here I was, apparently lacking my peripherals, searching in the figurative dark for these combustibles that Eric had ordered me to purloin. If my mom had been there, she'd have been taunting me to the point of my actually going blind from sheer embarrassment. Yet unless I could summon exotropia at will, I would have to use whatever peripheral vision I did or did not have to lock onto the cigars and gas, which I now stood in front of. Eyesight at stasis, feeling bold, with one fell swoop, I grabbed both the fluid and smokes. The cigars came off nice and easy, but the lighter fluid snagged on the rack. My adrenaline shot up, but I calmed enough to *slowly* pull the fuel from its hanger. I then stuffed the items into my coat pockets, hunched myself over, and peered around erratically like a paranoid schizophrenic. From there, I walked a couple of aisles over and approached Eric; he patted me on the back, and we walked toward the exit.

Easy! I did it again. Two successful, badass big-time burglaries. Who's the man? I'm the man, the man who steals shit! I was now experiencing yet another new series of sensations—control and power. Eric would definitely have to stop treating me like a subhuman and start respecting me now. Maybe I could get him to stop hating Jews too? How could he not? I, a Jewish guy, pulled off two perfect pilfers in one single day. He got everything he asked for, the way he wanted it, and I was the one who did it—with skill to burn. How could he hate a Jew if said Jew was totally subservient to him? And totally rad. I really felt as if I was making some sort of ceremonial transition from punchable dork to kiss-ass dude. I assumed every emotionally and physically hazed nerd had to do something like this to become cool, to break on through to the awesome side—as if it were a rite of passage.

As we reached the threshold that would transfer us from the drugstore to the parking lot, I felt as if I was about to taste freedom. That was when I felt a large hand hit my shoulder with the type of strength only an adult, or medium-size gorilla, could apply to a kid's body. I froze as this adult, or perhaps ape, turned me around. I was at eye level with this human's, or perhaps anthropoid's, waist. I craned my neck upward, as far as it could go, and locked eyes with the tallest, scariest-looking human drugstore manager I'd ever seen in my entire life. At the time, he seemed ten feet tall, though in reality he was probably around five foot nine. Keep in mind I was but a shorty.

"Can I ask what you have in your pockets?" said the sky-high manager guy with a gravelly voice.

I looked to my right; Eric was gone. The manager still had his massive hand on my small shoulder. I timidly reached into my pants pockets and turned them out. Nothing. The manager looked more disappointed than a human being possibly could. Again, up until then I was a big-time rule abider, so I'd never really seen true disappointment. The manager sighed—beyond annoyed.

"Your *other* pockets," he said with the seldom-used, but incredibly balanced, combo of calmness and impatience—calmpatience.

The jig was up. I was on my own. I didn't have my "protector" with me, Sir Hates-Jews-a-Lot. In an instant, I lost all the undeserved confidence I had built up from stealing crap and reverted back to the good boy, the rule follower, I naturally was. I removed the stolen items from my pockets and handed them to the manager. He then returned the favor by grabbing my shirt collar and leading, not dragging, me to a back room.

Here's where realization meets stupidity—once inside the security office, I saw through the one-way window out onto the floor of the drugstore. Minutes earlier, while I had been practicing my browsing, I had looked up and noticed an ominous opaque black window. I couldn't see into it. I had not considered it a window at the time. It was just a large black rectangle embedded in the wall, near the ceiling—a totally normal thing to install in a store, I thought. I didn't know why it was there, and I didn't really care. It didn't register. I shrugged at its existence and went back to what would turn out to be a failed caper. But now that I was standing on the other side of the black window, I felt like a giant fraud.

Not too long before my apprehension, maybe a week or so earlier, I had rented *Marathon Man* from Star Flicks. My dad had recommended it; he made it a point that I should watch a lot of classic films, not for any reason other than that they were classics. Now, at this very moment, after being led up a small flight of stairs by the collar, I was sitting in a darkened room with a couple of Compaq Presario computers and a monstrously mad manager with his arms crossed, sitting on a stool, staring at me with eyes so piercing they could slice flesh from the bone. I searched around the room for dental tools and was relieved to see none—he wouldn't be drilling me for information. What other form of torture would the manager use to extract data from me? Would I survive? I was sweating again. A swell of emotions—fear, shame, guilt, embarrassment—pulsated through my being. My asthma, which I took poor care of, kicked in. I was taking short, fast breaths, due to both bad lungs and anxiety. The air seemed to have literally been sucked from the room.

"You know what you did was very wrong," the manager scoffed.

"Mm-hmm," I fearfully agreed, shaking my head, gasping.

"You know I could call the police. I *should* call the police."

As the manager threatened me with due process, I could do nothing. I was suspended in animation as my life flashed before my eyes: I was born, I had a dog, he died, and now this. I didn't have a specific pop culture reference at the time for how I knew prison was scary, but I knew it. It's prison. And that's where I was going, and that was that. No more staying up late to watch *Beavis and Butt-Head, Mr. Show, Mad TV, Pinky and the Brain*, or *Johnny Bravo*. No more SpaghettiOs with meatballs where I could just eat the tiny horse meatballs and leave the gelatinous Os. They probably would just serve the Os in prison. And I'd have to watch the news with all the other prisoners, who would laugh at my tiny mushroom penis in the shower. This was all from a kid brain, mind you; adult me knows they'd *love* the tiny penis in the slammer; it would make it easier to visualize me as a woman. A huge plus for prison rape!

If I could've pissed my pants, I would've, but I was so thirsty, so devoid of moisture due to minor heat exhaustion, that I couldn't have pushed a drop out if I tried. My hands and knees trembled. The manager continued scolding me, but now his voice fluttered somewhere in the background, muffled, pitched down. The world slowed to a near halt. White noise swelled inside my head until it reached a deafening peak. Suddenly, the world sped back up, and I reentered it.

"Mess with the bull, you get the horns, kid," the manager said, so matter-of-fact that the old adage didn't sound trite but authentically frightening. Was I to get stabbed in the face with some sort of disembodied bull horn that this hulking behemoth kept around? And then the manager took a deep breath. I was ready. Stab away.

"But this time, I'm going to give you a break."

It took me a moment to comprehend what he had just said. I looked on, perplexed. The manager got up from his stool and resumed being much taller than me. I had half a mind to assume this Ivan Drago–sized human meant "break" in a very literal sort of way. The manager then put his hand on my shoulder and gently led me out of the back room, down the stairs, through an aisle, and out the front door. Standing on the sidewalk adjacent to the parking lot, we stood face-to-face, or more face-to-crotch.

"Let this be a lesson, kid. I let you off easy. But I'll tell you one thing: if you set foot in this store again, I will call the police. Got it?"

Wide-eyed and shaken to the core, I nodded fervently. The manager stood with his hands at his hips, looked me over once more, and declared with a single nod of his own that we were done here. He was off. That was it. I was now alone, with my humiliation and residual shakes. In a daze, I stood there for what felt like hours but was probably about five minutes. Then I set off on the three-mile walk home.

Back at my house, I felt cagey, exposed, like everyone knew what I had done. I pushed my cold dinner around for a while to make it look like I had enjoyed it, then stayed up until all hours of the night watching *Twilight Zone*, eating overcooked hot dog slices from the toaster oven.

The next day, at school, I caught Eric in the hall with his cohorts. I approached him to fill him in on what he had missed, the harrowing details of my capture and escape. I was planning on *really* hamming it up and making it sound like "I didn't take no shit from no one, ya hear?" I wasn't going to tell him how I would've pissed myself if I hadn't been so paralyzed. Or the fact that I could barely utter a noise, let alone a word, because I was so mortally terrified of the big, tall man. I mustered all my confidence, still assuming I had crossed the threshold from dork to in-crowder and would be welcomed into his clique.

"Eric, you wouldn't believe what happened after you left," I eagerly exclaimed.

To which Eric stepped toward me with an ever-so-gracious, "Faggot!"

I gather he ran through all the antisemitic slurs in his dinosaur pea brain, they seemed tired, and he opted for something fresher and more homophobic. Eric and his pals yukked it up, high-fiving as they walked down the hallway. I stood there, sullen, head down, like a budget Charlie Brown post–football fail without the accompaniment of the smooth, sad sounds of the Vince Guaraldi Trio. Once bitten, twice bitten, a thousand times bitten, and I kept coming back for more.

A week later, my mom had bought the *It* miniseries on videocassette to watch with me. That made-for-TV film came in a double VHS set, so we were in for a haul. And we were out of movie snacks; that was not going to fly with Mom, a staunch Twizzlers-with-her-films kind of gal. So we piled into the car and headed off to the snack-a-torium, with me blissfully unaware of our specific destination.

As we approached the drugstore, the same one I had been told to never enter again, I instantaneously became stricken with dread. I clutched my mom's hand tightly as we entered, something I (a) hadn't done in years and (b) knew she did not like or want. She coldly shook me off her, as Cathie was wont to do. Without so much as a mommy to comfort my barely contained woes, I shook uncontrollably, fearing I was about to be found out, maybe even arrested.

Here I was, schvitzing once more, a never-ending magazine of sweaty ammo, as I followed my mom, nipping at her heels, down the candy aisle. I peered up at the black rectangle for a beat, then back down, hoping not to draw attention to myself. My mom grabbed some Twizzlers bags, and I tripped into her.

"What are you doing?" she sharply asked, as if I were deaf, dumb, and dumber.

"S-sorry. I'm just *so* excited to watch the movie. Can we go now?" I sputtered out quickly and awkwardly.

We headed to the checkout counter. My eyes darted around, looking for the tallest man I had known, but no one came to snatch me into the dark back room. And then we left. There was to be no prison for me. The inmates at the penitentiary would have to go another day without my boy-gina.

Later that evening, back at home, my face affixed to the television as Georgie Denbrough reached his hand into the sewer drain to get his boat back from Pennywise, who in turn bared *It*s teeth, ready to feast on Georgie's fear and flesh. It dragged the boy down into the dark sewers of Derry, Maine. Mess with the bull, you get the horns, I suppose.

# Give Up the Punk

Aaron Gedge stood on the steps of Chagrin Falls Intermediate Elementary, coolly asking passersby if we wanted to hear his demo tape. I was somewhere between nine and ten years old, desperate to make friends and therefore *quite* intrigued by anyone desiring a moment of my attention. At this point in my life, my exposure to music was a combo platter of what my parents played in the car (Beach Boys, Motown, Aaron Neville, occasionally Allan Sherman's "Hello Muddah, Hello Fadduh") and what I gleaned from Cleveland's number one rock station, "WMMS, the Buzzzzz-arrrrrd!" The latter turned me on to the big bands of the '90s: Nirvana, Pearl Jam, Smashing Pumpkins, Soundgarden, and some lesser knowns like King Missile, the Jesus Lizard, and Green Jelly.

I believe it's incredibly important to know where your food comes from. And in a similar vein, it's good to know where your music comes from too. For instance, on a global scale, you should know that your favorite white rock acts stole everything from Black blues musicians—an obvious one. And on a micro scale, if you love bands like Green Day and Blink-182, then you need to go back and listen to the Damned and Buzzcocks. So here I was at nine, listening to all these big "grunge" acts with no clue as to what ingredients went into making their rock sausages. I was but a child, with no perspective, no older brother to shepherd me, and certainly no internet. But then Aaron played me his "demo."

He held his yellow Sony Walkman tightly, as if to keep a secret, and handed over the device's headset—those irritating gray plastic earphones that worked less to produce decent sound and more to chafe the outer ear. And as I donned the listening device and Aaron pressed the Play button, I was forever transformed. The music was fast, aggressive, snotty, and raw, yet also melodic and catchy. It was angsty. I felt angsty. At the time I was mostly on my own, building up a well of unmitigated disquietude and sadness, my only social interactions being intermittent shoves, sneers, or the occasional antisemitic epithets. This music sounded like how I felt inside. And it was *way* different from what I was hearing on the radio, which all came with a certain production value that felt . . . safe. Even regarding one of the biggest, noisiest, most influential acts of the era, Nirvana, if you were to go back to their first record, *Bleach*, and play it against *Nevermind*, you could hear in the former album the raw throw-and-go excitement that the latter does not have. And whatever Aaron was playing me had that excitement aplenty.

Now, these days, after twenty-plus years of professionally "musicking," I'm able to hear things in recordings that most people would ignore. I can tell you what type of guitar was used on this recording and what types of room mics were probably used for drums on that recording, and I'll be quick to correct you when you mix up the terms "autotune" and "vocoder." But even as an elementary schooler, with no professional musicking to boast, I knew Aaron was full of shit; this was not his demo, or any demo, for that matter. First off, it was too good—the record, the performances, and just the overall concepts were too mature and well executed for any nine-year-old to achieve. As I listened on, it became abundantly clear that this was a mixtape. For instance, song one and song two were audibly different bands, with completely different singers, who had clearly different voices. The production from song to song varied. Need I say more? Aaron was a fraud, a confidence man in training, a ne'er-do-well.

But I refused to call Aaron out on his fib. I didn't see this "deception" as cut-and-dried malice. I saw this act as authentic desperation, a yearning for human connection lightly obfuscated by his ruse. And I genuinely understood that dire feeling because I yearned for the same. We were both social pariahs—I, the unwanted Semite, and he, the adoptee, making it clear to me that he felt somewhat discarded by society altogether. And we both had this need to be seen, that want to be wanted.

However, my way of going about getting seen, and becoming wanted, was less steeped in fabrication. I vied for acceptance through what humorists would call crafting "old chestnuts." But every time I attempted to make a funny, my humor would almost always falter and backfire. See, I couldn't help but find myself *so* hilarious that I would prematurely chortle at my own bits. I still believe I'm worth laughing with, though most would exchange "with" for "at." So before giving anyone a chance to emit even a minor guffaw at my rib ticklers, there I'd be, bowled over, while my peers coarsely scolded me that it was *not* OK to laugh at my own jokes. And that admonishment would kill the vibe and send me right where I belonged, Shamesville, USA, zip code 9021-oh, bother. But Aaron, he didn't want me to go to Shamesville. He liked me just where I was.

I wanted to be next to Aaron too. I didn't want him to feel that humiliation and rejection I had allowed myself to endure, over and over. I wanted to let him off the hook for his minor subterfuge, trying to convince me he was both Ian MacKaye and Lee Ving all in one "demo." Aaron's horseshit ultimately came from a sweet place, that of needing a friend. And I needed one too. Plus, I wanted to know more about this music—this *punk rock*—and Aaron was to be my guide. So instead of being revolted by his deceit, I let him believe that *I* believed him, which felt mutually beneficial: the funny guy teams up with the punk aficionado.

Sitting in social studies, blankly staring at a wall projection of where the equator and the prime meridian meet in a sensual seaside African kiss, Aaron would sneak me CDs, the same ones he most likely used to construct his "demo tape." Through this, I amassed a borrowed collection of albums from artists like Quicksand, NOFX, and Fugazi; I still play these records today, on a regular basis. But without a doubt, the most crucial album, the one that set me on a musical path that would ultimately define my tastes, was Black Flag's *First Four Years*. This is not so much an actual album but a compilation of the band's early seven-inch records, a synopsis of their history before Henry Rollins joined the group. And while some of the songs on *First Four Years* came out as early as 1979, it felt, and still feels, fresher than most modern records within the rock pantheon.

As quickly as my obsession with Black Flag began, I leaped from their early, more straightforward records to their later, more experimental albums like *Slip It In* and *Loose Nut*. And that's when it all clicked, and I realized why all of my favorite "grunge" bands of the '90s would implement these off-key riffs and scuzzy, messy guitar parts. I finally understood where their intensity derived from, or at least what they were chasing after. And so because of Aaron and his itsy-bitsy hoax, I had been given the gift of sight. I now had this ability to analyze and ponder how and why a band would choose the sonic direction they chose. I began to care about the history of music, the "sausage making," which opened an endless well of musical discovery.

While I was posturing as a burgeoning musicologist, piecing together who my favorite bands' favorite bands were, Aaron and I were secretly plotting our own band. He had a drum set, and from my recollection, he could play fairly well. I, on the other hand, had a trombone. A rental trombone. And since we had yet to discover ska punk, thankfully, it was all on me to trade in my brass for something slightly stringed and a bit more electric.

But before I had ever pressed my lips to the ol' sliphorn, my parents had me playing a few different instruments at various locales. It started in first grade, taking piano lessons from a friendly blind woman who resided in a dilapidated horror house full of stray cats. This was, of course, my mom's idea. I would not recommend handing over a child's first musical pursuit to a ninety-year-old, milky-eyed piano teacher with the ability to stare both over one's head and into one's soul, thus instilling a sense of otherworldly doom. Her derelict Gothic house also teemed with the most intoxicating of odors: ammonia and fecal-matted pet hair. Every time we arrived, I would hesitantly trudge toward the woman's front door, as acute fear churned inside my gut. I don't know if I was more terrified of the wretched stench, which caused me to plug my nose for the hour, or if I was just afraid of those opaque Dead-ite eyes.

I never became good at piano. And soon after escaping from that stinky Texas Chainsaw house, I started playing viola in the school band. Not as small as the violin, not as chunky as a cello, viola felt like a nice, middle fit for a middle-of-the-road musician. But as it turns out, viola is very hard, and not easy on the wrists. I have delicate wrists, so sue me! Like a young Albert Brooks, I complained and ouched my way through never really playing the instrument. But I'm not sure if anyone noticed the lack of practice I put in. Because, when it came time for the holiday performance, or the Christmas performance, as it would have been called back then, I just lightly hovered the bow over the instrument, pantomiming, as the other students performed a rendition of "Jingle Bells" that sounded like all the blind woman's cats dying at once.

And with yet another instrument dropped, I decided to pick up the trombone. "Why the trombone? That sounds terrible," you boldly yet appropriately may ask. Well, it was the only available instrument left in the school band, and that was the only band in town. And I wanted to be in a band. So, always a glutton for punishment, I began my brass passage. All in all, I wasn't too awful at the trombone. I practiced the sheets and took it relatively seriously. However, soon after getting comfortable, I began to have trouble with the whole blowing-air-from-your-lungs-into-the-instrument element when, in the latter half of second grade, my asthma began to rear its air-usurping head. Despite the lack of lung capacity, I stuck with the instrument for a couple of years, until Aaron and I began scheming to start the gnarliest, oniest punk band in the South Russell / Chagrin Falls area.

Obviously, my next move was to beg and badger my parents for a guitar. Now, my parents were not thrilled that I had bailed on every instrument they thrust upon me. However, I figured that they would forget all about it if I just became adept at badgering them. And like the mighty badger, badger I did, over and over and over until my dad finally submitted. Well, it wasn't a complete submission. There were stipulations. You see, on top of being a barely adequate trombonist, I was also a barely adequate student. I preferred my grades in the lower Cs, upper Ds. And of course I wouldn't discriminate against an F. While my badger game was on point, my school game was so poor that it left my dad with no other choice than to dangle a guitar over my head to coerce me into achieving a solid B average.

I was pretty surprised my dad gave me any option whatsoever. The electric guitar isn't something most parents want their kids to play: it's loud (louder than a trombone) and brings with it a seedy element, a history steeped not just in rock 'n' roll but also in the sex and the drugs. But I'm sure my dad wasn't entirely too concerned about his third grader getting sexy and high. I think he saw this as an opportunity for both of us to get something we wanted and to stop me from failing school.

I discovered that achieving a B average is as simple as completing your homework, something I had never considered doing up until that point. I felt like I had really pulled one over on my old dad when he held up his end of the bargain and took me to a used instrument shop. *I got a guitar.* I was thrilled. And that specific guitar, well, of course it was not the most known, but it was the cheapest guitar in the shop! At least I could say that—which I did not. But I had to look at the bright side: I got a guitar, I guess?

Questionable guitar in my fist, Aaron and I started our band. But we never played out, nor did we have the guts to show anyone what we were doing in his parents' basement—*not* sex. No, we just endlessly performed the chorus to NOFX's "The Brews" until becoming tired and sweaty. We then left his house to throw rocks into a crick. Or was it a creek? Regardless, the flow of our friendship continued strong for the next few years as we bonded over punk rock, loneliness, dial-up porn (through my parents' America Online subscription), and playing secret shows, to only ourselves, in Aaron's bunker.

While I made some fair-weather friends here and there during my life span in Ohio, none were so steadfast, nor made such an impact, as Aaron. So when it was time for my dad to up and leave his position at the Cleveland Clinic, moving our family a mere six hours away to Illinois, I was devastated. Sure, rural Ohio wasn't a very kind place to us Jews. And looking back on it, the education and facilities we had access to were abysmal. But the factor at the forefront of my mind, which took precedence over all the bad, was my love for music and my best friendship. I didn't know anything better. The idea of leaving my best friend behind . . . it felt traumatic. It was the only type of loss I had dealt with up until this point. Without Aaron, I believed that I'd be alone from here on out, my punk rock journey becoming a sad solo act. So with my very long chain wallet packed away, a Minor Threat tape jammed into my own Sony Sport Walkman, and my junky guitar stuffed loosely into the back of my mom's Toyota 4Runner, I began the process of mourning Aaron Gedge and our punk rock fellowship.

Perspective is everything. And it took me less than a week to realize that Winnetka, Illinois, was a significant upgrade from small-town Ohio. We now lived a stone's throw from a real, major city, a place with no shortage of culture. And my family could rest easy, leaving behind the rejection we faced for not

fitting into a *Leave It to Beaver* mold, where townsfolk surely
wondered just how in the dickens we seamlessly hid those
pesky horns in our hair! And for the first time in my life, I was
surrounded by Jews. No one wanted to fart on me while pro-
claiming, "Gas chamber!" Things were looking up, and if I was
going to get called a "faggot" again, it surely wasn't going to be
followed with the word "Jew."

No, for one hot minute I was not an outcast but an interesting curiosity: the new kid. Everyone wanted to know the new
kid. Was he cool? Was he smart? Was he suave? Was he good
at Rollerblading? Obviously, I was none of these, but I tried to
live in this moment of pseudo-popularity for as long as it would
last. Girls even approached me. Real-life girls! They wanted to
know who I was and what I was all about. Now, *this* was frightening because I feared the opposite sex greatly. I don't think
one female had ever entered my personal sphere, by choice,
who wasn't a mother, grandmother, or the occasional unhinged
aunt.

Now that I was newly aware of my depression, self-depre-
cation was becoming my internal and external go-to for
everything. So it was easier for me to think I wasn't worthy
enough for the fairer sex than to risk any more damage to my
paper-thin ego through potential rejection. And this lack of
self-esteem was further bolstered by my mom having served
me a healthy portion of body dysmorphia, courtesy of comments such as "I mean, you are getting fat."

Anyhow, as the girls would eagerly approach me, wanting to
know the man *behind* the man, I had an internal parts breakdown, unable to compute the complex theories of "Flirt,"
"Talk," or, "Just say something, man!" So I stuttered my
way toward week two of middle school, organically shifting
from intriguing and potentially kissable to fully weird and

ignorable. But this was still an upgrade from my previous status of human punching bag/turd boy. And with the "new kid" sheen dulled and no friends to count, I fell back on the only support system I had: punk rock.

Years passed, and I found my niche by my sophomore year of high school. By then I had met and become accustomed to the North Shore brats. Sure, some dabbled in punk, but they preferred to retreat to their parents' six-bedroom quasi mansions to throw pseudo-parties with other brats, less interested in the Vandals and more interested in knowing where the vodkas and vaginas were being kept. I had the "pleasure" of starting my first band with some of these moonlighters, a hardcore band called Voices Still Heard—a generic name with zero meaning.

We were not great. I know I was not great. We recorded a demo tape, something I have intentionally lost and hope to never recover. At one point, we even tracked a song in the basement of a young recording nerd, Sean O'Keefe, who, funny enough, would go on to record Fall Out Boy's second indie album, our breakthrough, *Take This to Your Grave*. But outside of making abysmal music, we mostly listened to Hatebreed, a Connecticut hardcore band that had recently released what would become a classic album, *Satisfaction Is the Death of Desire*. It was clear that if this was the new standard, it might be better if we just stopped doing whatever it was we thought we were doing. Better for ourselves. Better for the world. Better for humankind.

And so by my sophomore year, again with no real friends, I realized it was futile to think I could make any headway in punk or hardcore on the North Shore. While my family had eked our way from a staunchly middle-class lifestyle to this newer, glossier upper-middle class, I could not identify with the type of uber wealth these rich kids dragged along every-where they went, like specters rattling their chains of affluence in my face. And it's not that I saw punk rock, or my new inter-est in hardcore music, as something synonymous with a spe-cific social status; it just didn't feel right to forge my interests in an area that favored opulence over character. I began to see the North Shore and rural Ohio as two sides of the same homog-enous, boring coin, full of people too self-involved and unin-terested in building a broader community. The last time I had felt any sort of community was when I was with Aaron, listen-ing to records, poorly but happily playing one NOFX song. I was in desperate need of connection yet again. But this time, I had options. I had Chicago.

To me, the Fireside Bowl was Chicago's CBGBs, *our* quintessen-tial, ramshackle punk venue that hosted performances by some of the most influential artists of the genre. The Fireside was a dilapidated bowling alley that at the time was not functioning primarily as a bowling alley. The derelict space held around five hundred people, meaning that by today's standards, it shouldn't hold more than about fifty people, safely. This venue was where all the best punk and hardcore bands would play—Dillinger Four, Refused, Buried Alive, Converge, Cave In . . . the list goes on. I can't keep count of all the amazing shows I saw, and played, during the Fireside's tenure.

Unfortunately, these days it's been rehabbed and functions primarily as a bowling alley once more; no longer is it a hole-in-the-wall dump factory for seeing the scene's most promi-nent punk and hardcore bands. It's been many years since this shift, and I still have a hard time reconciling the change, as both a punk kid (at heart) and an avid bowler. I think the Fire-side's owner got sick of screaming at people for smoking cigarettes out front between sets and wanted to live the easy-by-comparison life of running an upstanding no-cig, brawl-free establishment rather than wrangling apathetic pseudo-adults whose development arrested around age thirteen. As an ex-youngling turned aging man, I get it, as depressing as it all is to witness your youth slowly being strangled to death.

Speaking of youth, the moment I turned fifteen I began to seek out shows in the city. And somehow, I gained my parents' trust, just enough that they would allow me to traverse Chicago's public transit on my own. Keep in mind that, at that time, the area surrounding the Fireside Bowl was not yet the yuppie, button-down belt it is today, as it was overrun with gangs and extreme violence. It's not that my parents didn't know that was the case, but to what extent? Yet they clearly felt I could handle myself. Part of me looks back and thinks, "Maybe that wasn't very responsible?" But the other part is sincerely grateful for the opportunity and trust they bestowed upon me.

My first show at the bowl, I remember walking past a green sedan parked outside. I don't know why I took notice of the car; it was nothing special. I don't even remember who I saw play, but I know I had a blast at the gig. Then postshow, I exited the venue to see that the same green sedan had *also* had a blast—it had been firebombed. I made sure to hide that tidbit from my parents.

Firebombed at the Fireside or not, I was undeterred from spending as much time as possible there, or wherever else shows were happening around the Chicagoland area. During the day, I'd treat my time in high school as work; I'd clock in and clock out, making little eye contact, keeping my head down and my nose to the grindstone. At night, I'd take the train into the city and go to shows. And while I had an impossible time finding one friend at school, I ended up making not one but dozens at these shows, specifically with people entrenched in the Chicago hardcore scene. These were people from different backgrounds than my own, who came together under the collective notion of not just a love for music but a need for community. And to this day, I am still incredibly close with many of these people. Most were older than me; like big brothers and sisters, they took me under their wing, never treated me as subordinate, guided me through their world, and allowed me to be a part of what was ultimately a very encouraging environment. Sure, hardcore shows are full of violence. But it was a mutual violence. We beat the shit out of each other in the pit, then hugged it out afterward. A healthy release of aggression, never meant for anyone who didn't want it, save for the rogue neo-Nazi who would show up here and there, well deserving of every punch and fire extinguisher to the head.

Through my time in the Chicago hardcore scene, establishing some of the most important relationships of my life, I developed a new sense of self. And this was another pivotal moment of my musical trajectory. While I never had aspirations to become some big-time chest-puffing famous rock-and-rollsman, I was dead set on becoming further entrenched in the Chicago hardcore scene, by means of either starting a hardcore band, a good one this time, or joining an existing one. Local bands—like Extinction, Racetraitor (an anti–white nationalism metalcore band that informed many of my left-leaning social politics), and the Killing Tree—were admired greatly. Even though I put these bands on pedestals, the people *in* the bands were down-to-earth, regular guys (not many gals at the time; progress is a bastard) who became my mentors. That was one of the most extraordinary elements of that scene: everyone was surprisingly approachable—there were no rock stars.

So I hung around, hoping to eventually sneak my way into one of my new friends' bands. But as punk and hardcore bands are wont to do, all these aforementioned groups, and many more, quickly broke up almost as soon as they started. But there was no need to fret, as the guys from each group would always get together to form new bands, usually the next day. And it was then, around age fifteen, while the Pangaea that was Chicago hardcore broke apart and resituated itself into yet another formation, that I began to situate myself into a friendship with someone I'd end up spending the rest of my life with, Pete Wentz.

Pete had been in both Extinction and Racetraitor, and to a measly kid like me, he was Chicago hardcore royalty, a term so heavily ridiculous to scrawl out that I may have given myself a hernia in doing so. Yet it felt true at the time; I looked up to Pete. Many did. And right as he and I were becoming fast friends, Pete had started this new band, Arma Angelus. I remember getting their demo CD and placing it into my multifaceted, all-in-one CD/tape/radio boombox. The music that blared out of the tiny speakers was reminiscent of one of my favorite groups, Carcass, the English band whose '93 album *Heartwork* is undoubtedly one of the best metal records ever made. So parroting Carcass riffs made Arma Angelus my new *second* favorite band.

As a superfan (I was insultingly referred to as "Number One Fan" for a spell), I would go to every Arma show I could. But I never assumed my ultra-fandom would amount to anything more than the sheer pleasure of getting to see those guys play show after crushing show. About a year or two into Arma

Angelus's existence, they had made their first full-length album, *Where Sleeplessness Is Rest for Nightmares*. Now normally when a band makes an album, said band goes on tour to support said album. While a big, Fall Out Boy–type tour is set up by the great powers that be (i.e., booking agencies, managers, major record labels), a DIY hardcore band has to book a DIY tour on their own dime—usually leading to an odyssey that is janky and wholly unreliable.

So Arma did just that, setting up a short East Coast and southern US tour. But right before they were about to set out, their bassist, Chris Gutierrez, couldn't get time off from his paying job (the same Chris would later get immortalized in the Fall Out Boy song "Grenade Jumper"). Keep in mind, this was do-it-yourself; no one was bringing home money. The whole enterprise rested on getting all drill sergeant on that ass and making it work, come hell or high water, like the grab-ass-tic pieces of amphibian shit we were.

I don't fully understand how what came next transpired, but Pete asked me to fill in for Chris on bass. Now, consider a couple things: (a) I'd never been in a real band, (b) Pete knew I played guitar but had never heard me play, (c) a guitar is not a bass, and (d) I was five years his, and the rest of the band's, junior—I was but a high school freshman. I got past points a, b, and c by simply feigning both confidence and ability. Then point d, the age point, that was tough. But considering my parents were letting me freewheel around Chicago unsupervised, I figured I'd at least ask them about this whole "letting me traverse the country with a bunch of dirty twentysomething strange dudes" thing.

They said no. And then I told Pete, "They said no." Now, I do not know why Pete went out of his way to make the next thing happen. He must've liked me enough, or there was no one else available. Pete went to my parents' house, sat down with them, and Svengalied my folks into allowing me to go on tour with Arma Angelus as their temp bassist. To this day, Pete is still one of the most charismatic, convincing talkers I've known. He's just as good now as he was then.

A week later, I was to go on the first tour of my life with a group of unencumbered adults. We were to show up to basements, VFWs, and other shoddy venues in hopes that our shows were booked. I was also going to go through the worst hazing of my life, a true induction to the nitty-gritty of the touring world. While that sounds horrible, and sometimes was, it was one of the most transformative moments of my life. It forced me to go through a transfiguration, growing rapidly from a greasy, pimply, sheltered, naive child into a hardened, slightly older, acne-scarred child with a sheen of cool indifference. And even greater than the growth itself would be what would eventually come from the haphazard tour. As I mentioned earlier, local punk and hardcore bands don't last long. And soon after that tour, as Arma Angelus started winding down, or breaking down, Pete and I began discussing a newer, differenter band.

# Warped Speed

I don't know if anyone in a band likes doing press interviews, but I certainly don't. Outside of a few of the more upper-echelon rags, most publications seem to employ these fresh-faced, straight-from-the-womb journalists—still wet with amniotic fluid—bringing only boilerplate questions to the table. And the most tedious, repetitive, trite, and just downright mindless query is the ever-present "So what's, like, the craziest thing that's ever happened on tour?" You'd think after two decades of my being in a band, one that has graced the covers of almost every music magazine known to human existence (if that's even relevant anymore), this gossip grab would cease to enter my orbit—as it's monumentally bush league. And yet this line of inquiry manages to sneak its way into nearly *every* interview. Texas Instruments could not manufacture a powerful enough calculator to compute and determine the number of times I've answered this question with an equally boilerplate, brain-dead "Uhhh."

To further expand on how tepid, yet overcooked, this inquest tends to be, here is a very real math equation to elaborate:

*Twenty Yrs Fucking Around on a Guitar*
  *+ One Thousand Beers*
  *× a Bajillion Amt. of Drugs*
  *− Millions / Hrs Sleep*
  *= I Don't Ever Know Where I Am Right Now or*
  *Was Before, K?*

Now, listen, I get it; these people are trying to make a name for themselves in journalism. They're looking for Fall Out Boy's "Jagger and Bowie suck-fucking" or "Zep and the vagina shark" or "Nikki Sixx dying but then *un*dying" or "Ozzy eating/snorting bats and birds and/or ants." But to be an utter disappointment, I don't have that story. Yes, I've had my struggles with drugs, volleying between uppers and downers (Oxy-Contin and cocaine, the touring musician's brunch), trying to maintain a balance of numbness and "tight chill" to avoid confronting my demons. But I don't think society is as interested in glamorizing drug addiction in these modern times.

And, of course, I've had sexual encounters on the road. I was nineteen when Fall Out Boy started gaining popularity; what horny teenage boy in a "kinda sorta almost big" band would turn down uncomplicated consensual sex? But even these experiences were few and far between; I can count them on both hands, double it, then halve it twice, then perhaps remove a finger. These exploits were relatively normal—a guy on top of a girl, a girl on top of a guy, a guy behind a girl, a girl more or less over it. If anything, describing the sexcapades in fifty or more shades of gray would be borderline gross and/or weird and/or also slippery while uneventful. So on the cool drugs and sex stories, I'm a zero-for-two type gentleman.

Regarding the whole aforementioned "time plus intoxication equals forgetting" mathematical construction, it's not entirely true that I don't remember significant events during my time with the band. It's just that I don't recall things that are mundane, which to me are the majority. I understand that the idea of being in a touring rock band seems wild and fun without a dull moment, but that was my day-to-day life. Consider being a part of a traveling sideshow circus: it's only a sideshow to those ladies without beards and boys sans lobster claws.

I do remember things. Important things. Transformative, critical things. Fall Out Boy things. Moments that led to etching the band permanently into music history, for better or worse. It still blows my mind, every day, that this thing I'm a part of, this band, is something that strangers are *very* familiar with and celebrate; it's a legacy, something that may very well exist beyond my death. I have yet to wrap my head around this concept fully, and I may never. It's not in my DNA to ride a high horse, be full of myself, or even celebrate my accomplishments. My self-esteem, measured in length, comes in at about a millionth of a billionth of a billionth of a billionth of a centimeter's millimeter's third cousin completely removed. The upside is I'm bad at narcissism. But because I'm aware of the weight that Fall Out Boy carries, it's impossible, no matter the amount of implicit self-hatred or substance abuse, to forget some of the crucial events in our career, the ones that felt like impossible, Sisyphean tasks.

So what ostensibly dense question would I prefer a journalist to ask of me? Simply put, "Do you recall the moment, *the* moment, when the band became big?" That may seem like an even more ludicrous ask. But if you're above the age of thirty, you most likely have enough time under your belt to recall those life-changing, pivotal moments over the day-to-day constant and mundane ones.

Yet as clear as day, I can recall the exact instant when Pete Wentz, Patrick Stump, Andy Hurley, and I went from "*Maybe we can make this last for another four to five months, tops*" to "Wait . . . are we a real band now?" The year 2004 had been filled with a series of payoffs after four years of relentless, brutal touring: driving a windowless cargo van with faulty brakes, performing at bars for only the local venue's sound guy, sleeping next to cat shit in trailer homes, traveling in an eight-passenger van with no air-conditioning that barely huffed and puffed its way across the country as rain leaked through the shoddy doors. We almost drove off a cliffside crossing the Rockies in that van. That same tour, I watched someone die in another person's arms, the aftermath of a brutal road accident, as I hauled fourteen hours to a gig, fueled by trucker speed, dirty bean water, and Jolt Cola. The unfortunate combination would challenge my pelvic floor while I clenched my anus desperately, mental fortitude and youth the only barrier holding back an onslaught of slippy, sloppy diarrhea.

With all that in the proverbial rearview, we were now living large, by comparison. Our van had grown, from an eight- to a fifteen-passenger vehicle—something that could haul a sizable trailer, enough to safely carry our gear and merchandise comfortably. Despite being the emo-punk lepers of the scene—we had extreme difficulty getting on any tours—we had beaten the odds and amassed a surprisingly ardent following. Part of that had to do with the album we had been touring on, *Take This to Your Grave*—recordings cobbled together with the help of a friend's ten-thousand-dollar loan and an upstream record deal between indie label Fueled by Ramen and major label Island Records.

Though the album cycle for *Take This to Your Grave* started slow, a year or so into grinding on the road, smashing those songs into people's faces, the music caught on; the record started doing well, selling thousands of copies a week, incredible for an independent record in the early aughts. And it didn't hurt that, in the crafting of this album, Patrick had quickly honed his skills as a songwriter/music leader. Plus, we had access to Butch Vig's late and great Smart Studios in Madison, Wisconsin, along with the matchless guidance from the aforementioned Sean O'Keefe, a fledgling producer and one of the few people at the time who believed we had music worth recording.

Another factor in our initial success, a spark that has unfortunately waned in our elder years due mainly to chronic and degenerative injuries, was our unbelievably intense performance in our live shows. While Patrick would be anchored front and center, singing blue-eyed soul over four-chord punk rock, Andy would rigorously hold down the kit with a focused, animalistic intensity (a Dave Lombardo–meets–Animal type), and Pete and I would bound about the stage, focused only on swinging our bodies around like two halves of a hulked-out Iggy Pop after guzzling ten pints of Pete Townshend's piddle. Rather than play the instruments as they were meant to be played, we used them as ornaments while we jumped off walls, into people, off people, onto people, into people again, then off balconies and onto people, then off balconies, missing people and hitting floors next to people—anything that leaned toward death-defying, budget Evel Knievel material.

Looking back at old footage of myself, it was as if I were the physical manifestation of full-blown hypermania, though it's clear now that this acting out was my way of releasing all the negative energy I had stored up from years of trauma. Losing myself in the process, rather than dealing with the pain I had endured from the verbal and emotional abuse at the hands of my mom, allowed me to put 100 percent of myself into the production. Of course, in retrospect, I wish I had put that negative energy into playing my guitar rather than chucking it around like a Tilt-a-Whirl manned by a gakked-out carny. While I've become a student of the craft since those days and have some residual shame for not being a better player, I don't regret approaching our live shows in an utterly chaotic, slapdash manner.

Lots of bands sound great live. When Fall Out Boy was coming up, there were countless groups in the local Chicago scene tighter than newborn dick skin stretched across an Olympic-sized pool. But we were sloppy as all hell. And yeah, it didn't help that our first three drummers, before Andy, were the polar opposite of a metronome—a metro-nope. But we wanted to stick out, and given our hardcore roots, we didn't think live shows were about being pitch-perfect. They were about expressing one's emotional state through being physical—stage diving, head walking, throwing your guitar around like an asshole. There were no James Browns in hardcore, fining band members for every flubbed note and missed beat. When it came to live performance, we only knew visceral aggression, full-body flailing, and hefty audience participation—if you were at the show, you were part of the show. One of my earliest reference points for that was Kansas City's Coalesce, a band that would literally throw their amps at people; you listened to their records for the songs, but you went to the shows for the excitement and participation. And to get hurt. There was an element to hardcore music that entailed tapping into whatever pain you held on to and letting it out sideways. And the crowd would reciprocate à la primal group therapy.

We wanted early Fall Out Boy to take that hardcore energy, the exposed, emotional rawness, and transport it directly into our live shows, as if we were the heaviest, hardest band in a scene that was neither heavy nor hard. And we did that. From 2000 to whenever we got too old to perform as Cirque du So-lame (2013-ish?), our shows were frenetic and constant from note one. This created fervor, which molded interested parties into fans, then converts, until by late 2003, early 2004, the crowd belonged to us, and we to them. This made for an intense shared echo chamber of kinetic energy; the more we cared, the more we moved, the more the crowd moved and cared. We fed off each other like vampires in an infinite suck fest of dynamic vivacity and emotional desperation.

So as *Take This to Your Grave*'s record sales ramped up and word got out that we, the emo-pop-punk pariahs, were packing house nightly, it became harder and harder to box us out of situations meant for only the "hippest," "coolest" bands on the scene. In retrospect, none of them were hip or cool. However, when we got a coveted spot playing a midsize stage, midday, at one of the most significant punk festivals of that era—the Skate and Surf Festival in Asbury Park, New Jersey—we knew it may be a moment, maybe not *the* moment but still a crucial step along our trajectory.

Bored by the drab, landlocked Midwest, I was excited to plant my feet on the East Coast. I desperately wanted to soak in what I assumed would be more urbane culture. Just four or five years prior, at fifteen, during my first-ever tour as the fill-in bass player for Arma Angelus, I was fortunate enough to spend some time in Manhattan. This was the late '90s, when the city was still dangerous yet exciting. Times Square was rampant with people ready to jackknife you outdoors, while seedy establishments lured you to jack off indoors.

Residing in my nature is the predisposition toward not just jacking off indoors but also putting myself in other precarious scenarios, a compulsion I inherited from my mom (not the jacking off part, Jeez Christ), who, at only twenty, decided to backpack, solo, across the African wilderness on a whim. This tale was always told with a sense of apathy, as if it were passé and not dangerous enough. And this is where we diverge, as my amygdala processes fear just fine, whereas hers was clearly stunted, coupled with the brain damage itself most likely hindering logic and rationale. But like my mom, I enjoy fighting my fears to see what rewards lurk on the other side. And so I was hyped to go out East, to Asbury Park, a place so close to New York City that I assumed it would be a sort of Manhattan-lite.

Asbury Park was mostly known for Mr. Sexy-Butt-Handkerchief McDenimman himself, Bruce Springsteen, and his guitarist, Tony Soprano consigliere and DiMeo crime family associate Stevie Van Zandt. But it turned out not to be the big-city-adjacent cosmopolis I had naively envisioned it to be. Upon my arrival, I was greeted by a dismal place, a city ravaged by racism and socioeconomic disparity. It reminded me of an oceanside Detroit. And much like Detroit, Asbury has since seen somewhat of a resurgence. But at the time of my arrival, it wasn't safe to venture past the festival grounds. And there wasn't much to see outside of the convention hall where the festival was held; most of the neighboring structures resembled tenements, and I wasn't too interested in getting impaled by the urban homologue of a boar's tusk.

So we, the band, were stuck in this concrete relic of a venue. We had nowhere to go and nothing to do except bite our fingernails at the uncertainty and anxiety of our impending set. The Asbury Park Convention Hall was once a historic, prosperous venue that hosted everyone from the original lineup of Lynyrd Skynyrd to Mr. Sexy-Butt-Handkerchief McJeans-boy himself. But by that point, the place had seen better days; the monolith of sea-salt-damaged stone resembled a bombed-out, war-ravaged European edifice. Essential heat and air-conditioning were but a luxury, and the live audio could not be honed; it warbled around the venue, bouncing and reflecting off the untreated walls, creating a horrendous cacophony of noise. The festival's various band stages fought tooth and nail for sonic domination.

But I didn't care what the place was or wasn't; none of us did. All we knew was that we were in the company of some of the biggest bands from the scene—Taking Back Sunday, Brand New, Coheed and Cambria, the Starting Line—and we were fortunate to be playing in the same space. Fuck, even Joan Jett was there, something I should've been far more excited about at the time. For a group of medium-to-large-sized children, this felt like a chance to enter the big time with the big boys. In my mind, this was a door opening, and if we could success-fully maneuver through that door, perhaps we could finally be accepted into the cool-kids' club and be associated with these larger bands—to be seen as something substantial and real. In hindsight, this was a very myopic view, as this was just an emo scene bubble, one that has since burst and will never exist again as anything more than a relic in time.

The festival's main stage was situated in a large room con-taining a half-sized arena, the smaller stage in a cozy theater, and the midsize stage, where we were to perform, was set up in the venue's main hallway. All the merchandise booths stood in this airplane hangar–sized region, which thus acted as more of a pass-through for festivalgoers rather than an ideal setting for watching live music. And the stage itself, the one we were to play, was ten feet tall at a minimum, so you had to crane your neck just to see what was happening. Again, not ideal. As I mentioned prior, the sound in that arena was more or less a wash of indiscernible noise. And now we were standing behind this massive stage, waiting to go on, feeling a little cheated.

Having just watched another band play in the small theater, I wondered why we didn't get placed there. It was a decent-sounding room, compared to where the other stages sat, and it felt more suited to our size, as far as I knew it. I began to get nervous about our prospects of having an even *subadequate* show. I became fearful and rife with early-onset embarrassment, projecting a horrible performance and preparing myself for gutted disappointment. While I never stated these concerns aloud, I'm sure the look of terror on my face was contagious.

While the previous band's gear was being loaded off, the stage manager called for us to climb up the steep, rickety staircase to stage center—one of the shortest-longest walks of my life. Before arriving in Asbury Park, I had been so eager to play this festival, near these other bands. I had envisioned playing on an intimate stage to a healthy-looking crowd. But since that was out the window, all my excitement, joy, and confidence washed away in a panic as we climbed Jacob's ladder to what would be our eventual shutout from emo heaven, which is just hell, I guess.

I was still unable to see over the stage, and it seemed whatever crowd still lingered about was nearly silent. This was by no means library silence; there was the foot traffic and dissonance of echoing conversations from passersby most likely making their way to the main stage or heading outside for a smoke. But I could most definitely hear my own heart beating loudly—and it was intense. As an asthmatic, when I get anxious or nervous, the air escapes from my lungs; in those situations, it helps to have my inhaler. Luckily . . . oh, wait. Nope, didn't have my inhaler. OK, so now I was also struggling to breathe. This was a slow, meandering, dragging, Lovecraftian death playing out in real time. No turning back, though. The phrase "the show must go on" means "we are paying you for a service, so please render the service, or you will not get paid and also *maybe* not work in any town ever again."

My close friend Josh Newton would often say that for artists, showing people your art is a lot like getting up on a stage in front of a crowd, nude, yelling, *"Hey, what do you guys think of my tiny penis? Is it OK? Please say it's OK!"* So you'd think it'd be easier to show your embarrassing genitals to a sparse crowd. Or no crowd. But it's worse to discover that no one wants to see your shitty prick. And that was the harsh reality I was readying myself for. The only saving grace was that I didn't have to go it alone. And so as we took our final steps onstage, ready to meet a sea of nothing, we were collectively hit over the head with a "what the fuck?" stick.

From the front of the stage to the exit doors, the entire hallway was filled with people—people patiently waiting for us to hit the stage. I can't fully describe my relief, my elation, or the otherworldly, warm, celestial change that took place within my body. My dopamine and adrenaline shot up in tandem as every hair on my arm rose to attention. "Holy shit," I thought. "They want to see our dicks." I strangely don't remember whether we received any applause before striking those first chords to *Take This to Your Grave*'s opener, "Tell That Mick He Just Made My List of Things to Do Today," but I know from there on out the crowd went off and sang every word of every song in our fifteen-to-twenty-minute set. To this day, our

2004 performance at Skate and Surf was one of the best sets of my life. It was fun, it felt dangerous, and most importantly, by the end, I didn't care what the other bands, or the entire scene, thought about us. That crowd, which seemed like the entire festival, wanted us. And we had a blast together, as a singular entity. It felt as if we had cracked something new, something beyond whatever the emo or pop-punk or regular-punk or not-punk-at-all scene was. It was the beginning of what would become our own scene.

From there, things continued to ramp up for the band. While the performance at Skate and Surf made waves, showing some folks that *perhaps* we weren't fucking around, we were still nowhere near being able to call any shots. On a larger scale, we had yet to make any real impressions within the perpetually unimpressed music industry. Credulity—informed by *Revenge of the Nerds*, where a singular, electric performance with your fellow Tri-Lambs at the big Greek Games is all it takes to prove that you've got the goods—led me to believe that this one big splash would set us up for good. But here's the thing about the entertainment business, whether it be music, TV, or film: One great look can nudge the door open *just* enough to slide a penny loafer's penny through. Then that door will continuously try to slam itself shut onto your foot. You have to push with all your might, over and over, to keep the door from closing.

Lucky for us, with the door ajar, another offer fell onto Fall Out Boy's lap—the Vans Warped Tour, a now-defunct traveling punk carnival that defined the genre for decades. In 2004, the tour was as strong and pervasive as it had been in the '90s, back when I had gone, as a fan, to the Chicago stop at the United Center's parking lot to see NOFX, ALL, and the

Deftones. The lineup in 2004 was no slouch either, consisting of the Vandals, Bad Religion, and, yet again, Taking Back Sunday (this was their era). So the opportunity was another biggie for us, a chance to play to new crowds and cut our teeth on the largest tour of the summer. Unfortunately, it was only five dates—a trial run. We were informed that *if* things went well, we *might* get asked back the following year. But at that time, we weren't deserving of anything more. And not being the types to bite hands willing to feed, we were off to get "warped," as they say. Or said.

Being a Midwest band, we were placed within a semi-midwestern part of the tour, a short run during mid-August starting in Hershey, Pennsylvania, and ending in Cincinnati, Ohio. The middle three dates were all in Canada, a country we had yet to play, and I genuinely don't remember much about those shows. The only thing I do remember is that we had brought a car to the show to easily get off the festival grounds and procure provisions (i.e., chips). At one point, I willingly attached myself to the hood of that car while Pete drove it twenty miles per hour and hit the brakes to see how far I'd fly. I look back at those moments and not only does the phrase "youth is wasted on the young" seem to come into clearer focus but so does why I had back surgery later that year. But at the time I felt totally fine after flying off the hood of a moving automobile and hitting a soft patch of pebbles and rocks.

Hazy, gravelly memories aside, the last two days of our short tenure on that year's Warped Tour are well embedded in my gray matter. August 15, 2004, we were set to play Detroit; and while the first date, Hershey, was fine, and the Canada dates banal, Detroit was something else. We figured it would most likely be a decent fare, considering we had a following in that area due to playing endless shows at the infamous venue the Shelter. This is the same Shelter where Eminem had once told a crowd to "lose yourself" in his "mom's spaghetti."

As festivalgoers began to gather in front of the tiny stage, it felt as if the show might be a good one. Eventually, a growing audience amassed to the point where they engulfed the dimensions of the platform, making it look novelty sized. After four respectable, non-earth-shattering gigs, we were more or less at home. And from the moment we took the stage, the crowd let us know by going absolutely apeshit.

We tore through our set, picking up frenetic speed, and every single person watching fed off that energy and returned it tenfold. Pete and I jumped into the crowd, smashing into people as we made room for others to get onstage so they could do the same. On and on and on it went. Like a human centipede of rock, not shit, it was hard to tell where we ended and the kids began. And as we collectively lost sight of our safety and gave in to madness, this amalgam of a thousand-plus people, rioting for the hell of it, turned the event from party-time USA forever to a full-on stage collapse. It turns out that everyone moshed, shoved, and stage dove so hard that they broke the platform's foundation. Now, to me, that's the sign of a perfect show—so long as no one is hospitalized or murderlated. Yes, the stage was toast, and so was our set, but going out in a blaze of "everything went wrong in the rightest of ways" glory did not just make four local yokels quite happy; it made an impression.

The next day, our last on Warped, we were victoriously "rewarded" with a spot on the main stage . . . at 11:00 a.m. To put that into perspective, we were set to play as the doors opened in the morning. This was both a "we see you" bonus and a "we also saw the damage you did to our property" fuck-you.

Normally, people in their twenties with questionable tattoos, dyed-pink hair, and long Dickies shorts don't show up in the morning. This was clearly punishment for breaking the stage, and also sort of a prank; the only thing missing was an era-appropriate Ashton Kutcher popping out to let us know that we were not punk but in fact had been *Punk'd*. However, like our Asbury Skate and Surf set, when we hit the stage, we were surprised by yet another large crowd gathered bright and early, just for us. Incredible.

As we dove into our early-morning set, I wanted to give thanks to that crowd, give something back by giving them a little piece of me. Naturally, I was going to stage dive onto those people, as if hurling my semisoft teen body onto perfectly kind strangers was any sort of thanks. But that was the ol' punk 'n' hardcore hug, and so I launched. Only I'd never dived off a stage that tall (it was at least ten feet high), nor had I attempted to clear a barricade, ever. After misjudging the fifteen-foot barrier by about five feet, I landed spine first on the steel barricade itself. The painful footage exists, somewhere, both on an out-of-print DVD we once released and on the World Wide Web. The ordeal was less excruciating than it was flat-out embarrassing. I walked it off, seemingly unscathed, as if my kid bones were made from rubber. And then, a few months later, I got the first of what would eventually be three back surgeries over the course of the next two decades, leading me to never dive off, or so much as move on, a stage ever again.

The following year, 2005, we were offered the entire Warped Tour—main stage, fully. Prior to this moment, the band had gone through some transformations. We nearly died in a horrible van accident, hitting black ice and skidding off the highway into a forest en route to shoot a music video. From there, we picked up the pieces and successfully made that upstream from Fueled by Ramen to Island Records, and we had *just* recorded and released our first-ever major-label album, *From Under the Cork Tree*. With no time to process the crash's trauma, and all the time to work, work, work, we had crafted an album that felt like the next logical step for the band, musically speaking.

From there, we were to choose our first-ever radio single—a daunting task. We'd never had to focus on singles or radio play until now, as we were an indie band working indie records, with no radio play. This was to be the first time we would attempt to release a song not to a scene but to the country. You only have one chance to make a good impression on America, and the single we chose to represent us was "Sugar, We're Going Down," a song that our record label, specifically the artists and repertoire (A&R) rep who had signed us, was certain would flop.

And so with this fresh record on the streets and wavering confidence at our backs, we started our journey toward what felt like a rite of passage—a full summer of getting very "warped," as I previously said "they" say. This entailed spending many hours, each day, in incredibly long meal lines to receive wafer-thin sandpaper chicken breast; receiving only Warped Tour branded lukewarm canned water to quench our everlasting thirst, full of nutritious aluminum flakes; and rarely getting a chance to bathe in anything less than three feet of septic water within repulsive porta-showers. That's something they don't tell you at Hot Topic!

Yet because I was young, dumb, and with my chums, none of this mattered, at least for the first few weeks. Except the not-showering thing. I sweat a lot, more than the average gent, whether I'm playing a gig on a hot summer's day or playing

*Donkey Kong Country*—my gorilla glands work overtime. They think they're cooling me off, but they're just making me sticky and disgusted by my own skin. I prefer showering on the reg, especially after playing music outside in temperatures of ninety-plus degrees. But no matter how gross I became, I refused to take even a spit bath in those filthy, clogged, biological disasters they offered. No, this was the summer of feeling like a peanut butter booger wedged inside a stinky plumber's butthole.

Personal hygiene aside, Fall Out Boy didn't feel ostracized on this tour, like we had in the past. We still felt like a bunch of newbs; Warped Tour had a little bit of an old boys' club vibe, where the been-around-the-block punk bands had their clique and got treated slightly better than us greenhorns. Fortunately for us, we weren't alone and were able to weather these cultural boundaries alongside the camaraderie of another younger, buzzed-about band on the scene, My Chemical Romance. Our bond on that tour was instant, as we both were navigating the same terrain at the same time; My Chemical Romance had just debuted their first major-label album as well and were waiting to see what, precisely, was supposed to happen next.

Regarding the unknown, whether our new single and album would make any impact, I couldn't seem to fret about it. I'm a constant worrier type, and it would have seemed apropos for me to agonize over the future of my career. But at this point, I was still treating the band as I had in the past, as something I loved doing for the sake of making music, something that afforded me the ability to drop out of college and not get stuck in a cubicle. I was counting down the seconds until impending doom. Since things had not yet become immensely complicated, I couldn't fathom concern. I just wanted to get on that stage and flail around like a rag doll with rabies, then cool off with some piping-warm canned water.

For the first few nights of the tour, I did my nightly stage thrashings to several thousand concertgoers a day. But then, after those first few gigs, something weird happened. You see, that single, "Sugar, We're Going Down," the one that was bound to fail, it did something quite different—it hit. It hit big. The following day or so, when we played the main stage, our crowd size didn't double, or triple, or quadruple, or quintuple. No. It wasn't even a crowd anymore, made of various sextuplets. It was the entire park this time, all fifteen thousand ticket holders gathered in front of the main stage, at our time slot, waiting to watch us play. This was clearly because our brand-spanking-new major-label single was getting proper play on the radio. This was the moment, *that* moment, the one where I watched us become a big band in *real time*. This was cause and effect in its purest form. I understood now what "blowing up" meant outside of domestic terrorism. And I felt that feeling: that cosmic, hair-raising, good-type-of-nausea feeling you get when everything doesn't just go your way—it goes your way plus you win the fucking lottery.

And wouldn't you know it, the same damned thing happened to My Chemical Romance too. Their single hit the radio, and every person in attendance would make sure not to miss a moment of their set either. So together, we became a dynamic duo that ended up drawing the entire Warped Tour in 2005. But the folks who ran Warped either didn't seem convinced this was real or wanted to knock us down from our newly anointed high. So in the days to come, My Chemical Romance and Fall Out Boy were placed on the main stages at 10:00 a.m. and 11:00 a.m. time slots, respectively, just to see if we were really worth our weight in shit. And sure enough, as the doors opened, the entire park filled up instantly to watch both bands. Then, once we both finished our sets, everyone left—the park was empty. Warped Tour's promoter *had* to accept a bit of defeat, as these two new bands that did not fit within their inner circle were indeed drawing the entire tour. From there on out, we both closed every Warped date essentially as the festival's headliners.

It was a strange and wonderful year that bonded us and My Chemical Romance, as we both learned to handle a sort of novel fame and notoriety. We became close with the guys, especially the Way brothers—two of the sweetest, loveliest, most genuine, and most creative people I've known. But they're all total mensches—something quite evident when one of my closest friends, Chuck, passed away from a heroin overdose, back in Chicago. As I flew home from the Alberta, Canada, date on Warped Tour for his wake, it was Ray Toro, My Chemical Romance's lead guitarist, who filled in for me, using his wizardly sight-reading skills to smash through the Fall Out Boy set, probably better than I ever could. I don't know if I could've made it through that tour without that support system.

Despite some of the issues (like low-grade pay and being forced by the promoter to play inane outdoor laser tag with festivalgoers as part of some confusing daily press scheme), I look back fondly on that time. It was truly momentous and defining for the band. You remember your firsts, the big ones, and I can't ignore that this was one of my career's most prominent. But Lord knows I'd never do something like that again. I can't go that long without showering.

# Hey, I Just Work Here

I t's odd. Odd that I can say, at thirty-eight, I've been a touring musician for twenty-three years. That's sixty-some-odd percent of my life. Sixty percent of my life spent more or less on the road. Twenty-three years. Now, a normal person with a standard nine-to-five kind of life might inquire, "How is that possible? That would have made you . . . fifteen? And well, that's just not . . . " Appropriate? No. It was not. And yes, I was a slight boy of fifteen, braced in the tooth, bespectacled, and bepimpled. I was an untouched, unchristened, speech-defected (lisping and stuttering), frenetic, nearly prepubescent fifteen-year-old when I did my first van tour—a squalid, dubious jaunt across the South and the East Coast, in a windowless cargo vehicle with the very person I would end up forming Fall Out Boy with.

As we know, Pete Wentz and I met at hardcore shows in the Chicago area not long before he, merely twenty at the time, convinced my parents, two adults pushing fifty, that touring with his band, the virtually unknown Arma Angelus, was kosher for their kindelah. I don't remember how he did it exactly. I'm currently sitting next to Pete on a flight. He said he doesn't remember either. Regardless, I do recollect his keen ability to win over not just my mom, who, let's face it, was never the patron saint of good judgment, but also my dad, who operated with a much better grasp of logic and skepticism.

Pete oozed charisma and, with impressive eloquence, could sell a shark on the idea that it's just as possible to breathe on land as in the ocean, you just gotta give it a go! I love that about him; it's a trait that helped push Fall Out Boy forward for many years. So given that ability to sell, coupled with his immense confidence and high-level intelligence, my folks were no match for Pete.

While I'm sure his gut said this was a horrible idea, my dad felt assured by Pete. Plus, he knew better than to cross his wife. Dad always called Cathie a "small woman with a big personality." He was being kind—the woman was downright frightening.

But I also think my dad believed that my mom knew me best. And she firmly believed I could handle the ordeal (i.e., tour). She wasn't wrong; I handled it. But I can't say I'd allow my own kids to do what I did at fifteen. Because that's insane, to allow your inexperienced, amorphous progeny to explore the world for the first time shepherded by a flock of unbalanced, unknown pseudo-adults.

Without going into precise moment-by-moment detail, that first tour I had ever done was easily one of the most difficult experiences of my young life. To start, our travel accommodations amounted to a windowless cargo van with no back seats. We used amplifier cabinets as makeshift seating, covering them with thin moving blankets. That was comfortable for about five minutes, until the various sharp aspects of the cabinets—the Marshall logos, the wood framing, the corners—began to reveal themselves, causing our asses to go numb, bruising our hips and backs. There was also no air-conditioning, which *really* helped to accentuate the collective odor of five different assholes and taints. Also, our brakes were going out.

We never knew when we were going to get showers, which, for Mr. Showers-Twice-a-Day Trohman, was a shocking revelation. Sleeping arrangements postgig were always up in the air. You never knew if you were going to be sleeping on the floor of a sparsely appointed condo, a party-till-you-barf Animal House that will not allow you to shut your eyes because they don't want you to, or a *Deliverance*-themed trailer with cat-shit carpets occupied by a seventeen-chinned Hutt-family mountain creature asking if you "wanna meet Mama."

Getting paid for the shows themselves was also not a guarantee, so there was legitimate concern when it came to having enough gas to get from one venue to the next. And then there were the fights, such as the one in the Publix parking lot in Florida, where we smashed two college-bound white supremacists after they violently shouted the N-word at one of our tour mates, causing us to leave them so, so bloody and brutalized I occasionally still have nightmares about that incident. But hey, that's just a day in the life for ill-conceived punk touring!

What made this initial jaunt most jarring for me was the hazing I received from some of the other guys in the group (who shall remain nameless). Strangely, I look back upon it all and feel that it was necessary, for my own growth. I truly hold no grudges. I have this off-color belief that everyone new to a touring environment can, and should, expect to be treated like complete dog shit. It's a rite of passage that many of us touring folk have gone through to prove we can handle what is a remarkably difficult way of living. I'm sure in today's environment, this gauntlet is run with more care, if at all, as internet tattletale culture, for all the good it can bring, would not allow for the things I went through. Perhaps that's for the better, because let's just say, during that run, that I was pissed on more than all the toilet seats in the continental United States. I was also berated, punched once, slapped a few times, pushed around, made to carry a lot of the gear, and basically forced through the punk version of what frat bros do to new pledges.

At first, I cried. A lot. I was but a kid, and so I bawled like a kid getting shoved into a locker after getting gut slugged, before getting called "queerbait." Lots of tears and snot. Ugly, slimy, gross, embarrassing stuff. At the root of it all, I thought that their treatment of me meant that I was entirely disliked and unwanted. Seems logical; it's the same treatment I'd received from other peers and is reminiscent of how my mom seemed to feel toward me, at times.

On the contrary, as I came to understand, it meant I was liked and wanted, however fucked up that seems. These guys were trying, in their bizarre way, to help me to level up, to be able to handle the low lows that are so often a part of touring. They wanted to see what I was made of and whether I could handle it. You won't learn to handle the bottom of the gnarled, grisly barrel by floating idly on a fluffy, white security raft of safety. So throughout the weeks, I learned how to toughen up, lean into the insanity, return the piss back to others (I have my own supply), and do what I was there to do with a smile: play bass poorly to around three people seven nights a week.

I had so much fun. The shows were a blast, despite the low attendance rates. Plus, I got my first fake ID in Times Square, years before the M&M's store opened—the twenty-five-thousand-square-foot shrine to candy you feel just meh about. The band also played CBGBs before it became a designer clothing boutique. I was thrilled to be a part of punk history—that is, until Chris, the person I was filling in for, took off work *just* to fly in for that show. Fucking asshole.

At least I got to witness two members of the headlining band shove a fist-shaped dildo inside a poor horny woman—in their van, in front of the venue, of all places! It was hard *not* to notice the act, since it was happening in broad daylight, right next to us as we were passively chatting. Why hide? "Do what you love, and do it proud *and* in the open" is someone's motto, somewhere. Ugh, I can't unsee it. Or unhear it. It was awful. I'm hoping it wasn't so awful for her. For me, I wouldn't want a dildo of any sort, especially one the size and shape of a green Hulk glove, inside *any* of my holes. But I guess that doesn't mean that others don't want a large fist inside one of their holes. Know what? I'm not going to speak for other people's holes. It's 2022. Do what you wish with your holes.

Wholly speaking, soon after that tour was done, I landed back in the North Shore of Chicago and was extremely eager to tell *everyone* at school that I went on a "cool" punk tour. But no one cared. Being "punk" did not up my clout at school. I had no clout to begin with. So I continued to go to hardcore shows in Chicago, where I did have a modicum of clout. And I continued to affiliate with Pete.

As the next couple of years passed, the two of us reached a collective disillusionment regarding the negative, tough-guy nature that the entire hardcore scene had shifted toward. This new approach to hardcore, or more an appropriation and revitalization of '80s New York City hardcore, involved having big, bad muscles, working out, and fighting each other on the regular. It wasn't *really* my bag, because I'm just a big, bad wuss. It felt both quasi-athletic and pain-ridden, two of my biggest turnoffs. And so, informed by its negativity and need for weight lifting, Pete and I began to shy away from hardcore to form a more positive, non-muscle-based group with melodic leanings—which would eventually become Fall Out Boy.

Many people know the story, so I think it's wise that I tell it with brevity. Pete and I wanted to start a pop-punk band. Not only were we fans of the genre, but that particular music scene seemed to be budding in its own revitalized fashion, eventually turning into what would be known as the swoop-haired, eyeliner-clad, sad-boy emo movement of the aughts. But until that moment crescendoed, Pete and I only had ourselves—with me making it clear I was the guitarist since it was my formative instrument and him taking the role of bassist since he had performed as such in many local hardcore bands prior. All that was stopping us now was the lack of a drummer and some songs. Oh, and a singer. Neither of us could do that, the sing thing. That's the hardest part, you know, of starting a band: finding a decent singer. If you don't have that, you don't have much at all.

And so, as the lore goes, I met Patrick Stump, by chance, at a Borders bookstore in Wilmette. I was with my friend Arthur, and we were flipping through CDs and came across Neurosis, the famed sludge metal band.

Arthur proceeded to ask, "Who is Neurosis?"

Before I could answer, we were approached by a fair-skinned waif of a teen with thick glasses and enormous sideburns—sideburns that looked like they had time-traveled, on their own, from an orgy in the late '70s to see what future fucking was all about. And this mutton-chopped urchin, he rolled right into our conversation and, unprompted, began explaining who Neurosis was. And my response to this obvious music nerd was to music nerd right back at him. I knew who Neurosis was. Nobody was going to out-Neurosis me, unless that person was Scott Kelly, the singer of Neurosis. Or other members of Neurosis. Or maybe their parents? I don't know.

And so as this hairy, elven man talked on, I talked on back. We both liked to talk, that was evident. We both liked to talk about music too. And we both seemed to like each other. We also both liked to *hear* ourselves talk. And as Arthur sank into the background, slowly morphing into an inanimate object, of sorts, Patrick and I clicked, phasing out the rest of the world so we could connect.

Within our barrage of musical conversations, or perhaps embattlements, I hipped Mr. Patrick Stump to the fact that I was starting a new band with this guy, Pete Wentz. Now, everyone in the punk and hardcore scene in the Chicago area knew of Pete. So Patrick was instantly delighted by the possibility of bestowing his talents upon this new Pete-helmed band. He offered his skills of drumming, bassing, and guitaring. But we needed a singer, I told him. And while hesitant to offer those services (Patrick has always been a reluctant singer), he nevertheless gave me a link to his MP3.com page (yes, that was a real website, before we knew the likes of Grüngle, Stopiphy, TreeFruit Music, and other cute monikers backed by supervillains). Energized, I immediately went home and listened.

The following day I called Pete over to my house to play him a demo by that pale, fuzzy guy who was going to be our new singer. Pete hated it. I relistened to the demo recently (courtesy of Patrick's hoarder-like propensity to keep *everything*), and I don't know what I heard then. Apparently, something. Enough to drag Pete to Patrick's house, where we forced him to sing and play guitar for us. In fact, we had Patrick play songs from what was our favorite album at the time, Saves the Day's *Through Being Cool*—a record that had a massive influence on

*Take This to Your Grave.* Where MP3.com failed, this live, awkward, uncomfortable on-the-spot "tap-dance for me, monkey!" performance won Pete over. It was clear from the start that we had just met our secret weapon, with an undeniable voice.

From there, using my bar mitzvah money to fund the band, we were off to the races, going through a barrage of drummers and second guitarists. And all throughout this embryonic stage of Fall Out Boy, where the only constant members were myself, Pete, and Patrick, I solidified my role as the glue guy, keeping us together, making us rehearse when no one wanted to, trying to push us forward when all felt hopeless, trying to make our terrible band good through sheer brute force.

But we were abysmal. We made bad demos. We then made an embarrassingly bad pop-punk time capsule of an album, *Evening Out with Your Girlfriend.* You may vehemently disagree with me, and that's OK. However, I will always consider it no more than a necessary horror. It's part of our history, but we hated it so much that we almost called the band quits. Then we pulled it back together, thanks to the fact that I pestered everyone to pull it back together through my superpower: annoyance. My voice can drone through *anything*, and I'm bad at giving up. I feel like a failure naturally, so I never want to feel like a double failure.

Eventually, upon reexamining some of our weak spots, we landed on two big changes: No more second guitarist; Patrick would be singing and playing rhythm guitar from now on. And we needed a good drummer. One who could keep time, perhaps. Maybe even an Andy Hurley type? He's the guy we wanted all along—easily one of the best drummers in the Chicago and Milwaukee hardcore scenes combined. Everyone wanted him in their band. I'm not even sure how we landed him in our early incarnation of Fall Out Boy. Did I mention we were abysmal?

Andy made us better. His solid backbone drumming made us want to be a better band. Soon after he joined the fold, we tightened the hell up and wrote new songs. Good songs. Songs we weren't embarrassed about. In fact, we were thrilled about them. Now that we had a real lineup, we felt like we had discovered our sound too. We just needed help recording said songs in a way that sounded good enough to hopefully land us a record contract. Lucky for us, others felt that same way, and we received some financial aid from a local pal, who I will refer to as Bill Givesalot. Bill received a windfall of cash upon his father's death and believed in what we were doing, enough to lend us thousands of dollars to record at Smart Studios in Madison, Wisconsin—the same studio where albums like *Nevermind* and *Siamese Dream* were made.

This led to three of the songs that eventually went onto our first real album, *Take This to Your Grave*. That record was then, and still is, pretty damn good. And at least one record label thought so too. Soon after tracking a portion of that album, we signed to what was once a little-known but well-regarded indie, Fueled by Ramen; finished the sessions; made the record; and toured the living hell out of it. But despite the quality of the album and the fervency of our touring, no one in the industry, outside of our small label and fledgling management, cared much for what we had going on. Luckily, we had the kids. All our burgeoning success at that time we owe to the fans. And we won those people over through not just that album itself but the consistent, hard touring, coupled with explosive, exciting, albeit *very* sloppy, live shows.

And as the kids followed, eventually the scene came too, as did the industry. While we were still somewhat outcasts, it was becoming clear that we couldn't be ignored much longer. The gates were being opened, and Fall Out Boy was welcomed into the music industry, though with some trepidation.

It was around this time when my role as the glue guy, the guy who was at least somewhat in charge, alongside Pete, began to waver. Things were getting a little more serious for our fun pop-punk band, as the inklings of a career began to appear in our future. And the more real these inklings became, the more I found myself getting lost in the tides of change.

Everything kept getting bigger. As the success of *Take This to Your Grave* propelled the band's popularity and upstreamed us from Fueled by Ramen to Island Records, the stakes rose, and the necessity to write new songs and produce an expensive major-label album became the focal point. Up until then, we were a down-and-dirty punk band, for better or worse, no matter how you may perceive us. Until that sea change, we were a united front, a motley crew, all on the same page. But as things began to grow out of the DIY and into the mainstream machine, my role in the band, as the person who kept us together and pushed us forward, was becoming obsolete.

I had helped write a bit of music on *Take This to Your Grave*— not a lot, but some. Patrick was, and still is, the band's main songwriter, innately talented at crafting hook-laden songs. Naturally, we lean on him for the bulk of our music. But I wanted to write more, to contribute my part. Problem was, songwriting was not something that came as naturally for me, at first. I had to hone that ability. By the time I caught up, it was clear I was too far behind. As the band's career moved forward at light speed and the need for new material grew, I found myself lost.

I wanted to contribute music and ideas, but I didn't know how to present them in a way that made sense. I really needed help. But I was too ashamed to request guidance, mortified that I wasn't producing songs properly, not the way I can today. I was quite young. I didn't know how to ask for what I wanted, not like a normal, healthy person. Instead, I asked like a tyrant pissant, pouting, stomping, passive-aggressively sneering, not understanding why me being a total drag wasn't working for anyone.

Dissecting that abhorrent behavior, I think my problem boiled down to the fact that, at one time, I knew who I was, within the confines of the band. But amid new adjustments, I was vacillating in the cosmos of Fall Out Boy, existing on the precipice between wide-eyed, hopeful excitement—that sort of feeling you get on the first day of attending a new school—and dark, dismal apathy—that sort of feeling you get on the second day of attending a new school. Things were about to go from pro-am to the majors for the group, and I was still stuck in pro-am mode.

The moment that the band progressed to Island Records was a paradigm shift like no other. Everything went into hyperdrive once we started production on what would become our breakthrough album, *From Under the Cork Tree*. And it was at that time that Patrick and Pete had begun to really solidify their sort of Lennon/McCartney duo, to share in each other's artistic spoils. This was the first time in our band's short career—four or five years in—that I started to feel a separation and was left to my own devices. So, flailing about, I began to desperately search for new ways into my own band.

We made *From Under the Cork Tree* in what would be considered an old-school fashion by today's standards of modern record production. We sat in a rehearsal space with Neal Avron, our producer, and played through songs that were mostly Patrick's music set to Pete's lyrics. However, apparently

I wasn't a total lost cause during these sessions. Patrick recently reminded me that I had helped to craft the verses of "Sugar, We're Going Down" and brought in riffs that became "7 Minutes in Heaven (Atavan Halen)"—small feats that didn't seem to register with me or make up for my insecurities at the time.

While at this current point in my life I feel content with my role and status within the band, back in 2005, I was beginning to feel both inadequate and worthless. I blame some of these feelings on the mismanagement of my own clinical depression. I allowed it to get the best of me, vomiting emotional bile onto everyone in my path. But age and inexperience play a large role as well. I've expressed publicly that I did not have the right tools to process my emotions during the early aughts in Fall Out Boy. While that's true, I am embarrassed that I felt the need to express it so publicly without having my head fully wrapped around the situation.

My behavior during the making of *Cork Tree* was rough, but things became even more foul during the making of our follow-up, *Infinity on High*, where I spent most of that recording process, and the tours themselves, consistently high on a combination of OxyContin and morphine, with heaps of bong rips to fill in the gaps. That was the bottom, an extremely dark moment in my life and career. I became a shell of who I once was, nothing more than a dismal drug dumpster.

Ever since I was a kid, I dreamed of being the lead guitarist in a rock band. And by that point, I had achieved it. But looking back on those occasions, when I allowed my pathetic self-pity to become entwined in every waking moment of my life, I wish I could have overcome my demons to enjoy those moments. I wish I had been more grateful for what I had at the time. There are so many bands that work themselves to the bone and never get one-thousandth of what we had then, or

Susan Averill
Catherine Babbin
James Bacon
Barb Baird
Ginny Baker

Martha Barnes
John Barnhart
Gregg Barton
Jeff Baumann
Patti Bearden

Todd Beel
Darlene Belcastro
Clark Bell
David Benedict
Steve Benedict

Michigan, 1960s. My mother's high school yearbook photo. You'll find her pretty face in the upper left-hand corner.

1985, Florida. Nope, that's not baby Shrek—it's a-me, Joe-i-o, less than two years old with a diaper full of poo. If only I knew then what I know now, I would've wiped that pompous grin off my tiny, stupid face.

Around 1988, Philadelphia. I'm aged four; my brother, Sam, was aged zero; and Mom and Dad were aged adult. My mom looks particularly thrilled here.

Early '90s, Ohio. No one seemed to care for my Pogo the Clown costume, neither my dad (left) nor my grandma Terry (right)—though my small potato brother (sitting on Grandma) seemed concerned, at least.

Late '90s, Illinois. My dad and I couldn't figure out where this pimply photo's from. It's not prom—I never went to a school dance. I'm not wearing a yarmulke, so it's not from my bar mitzvah. It might have been for an ad I placed in the paper reading, "Local nerd looking to get bashed."

# Who is the most double-jointed?

## Joe Trohman

Late '90s, Illinois. Probably the only time I was featured in a high school yearbook. Not sure about that look—somewhere between Ian MacKaye and Milo Aukerman. By the way, I am not double-jointed.

Late '90s, Somewhere, USA. Working on my scowl at fifteen. My first-ever tour with Arma Angelus and Seven Angels Seven Plagues.

I have to thank my pal Brandon Dermer for finding this gem from when his band, Cellar Door, opened up for Fall Out Boy (written incorrectly here) at the Winnetka, Illinois, Youth Organization in the very early aughts.

Early 2000s. Somewhere on tour with Fall Out Boy. A young boy but an old teenager. Credit: Pamela Littky.

I'm not sure about this athletic hooded vest situation, but I was then. However, I am currently sure I was bad at dressing myself. Credit: Pamela Littky.

Sometime around 2000-who-knows-when, when my dad and Chicago ska legend Roy Burgess became best friends for a spell. Probably taken at the Chicago venue the Metro.

Early 2000s. I'm maybe twenty here. Youth is truly wasted on the young. That shirt was a size small! These days I wear extra medium plus. Credit: Pamela Littky.

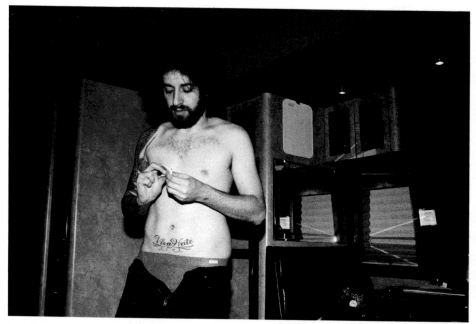

Local stoner displays male tramp stamp in the form of awful Morrissey tattoo. Taken on the ol' FOB tour bus. Credit: Pamela Littky.

That feeling when you're about to go on stage and play in front of thousands of people, and you're all like, "I am not qualified for this job." Credit: Pamela Littky.

If you put your ear close enough to this photo, you can hear me play "Aces High" wrong.
Credit: Pamela Littky.

The name of the song I was working on here was called "Dressing Room, Sweatshirt, Paper Towel, Laptop."

I guess this was the era when I owned three shirts and smoked three thousand cigarettes per minute. Gross. Credit: Pamela Littky.

As the old saying goes, "Time spent alone in catering, eating sad, dry cake and drinking a Diet Coke, is your awful business, man."

One of the few times you'll catch me genuinely smiling. Performing at the Whisky in LA with The Damned Things. I'm especially happy to be vibing with one of my favorite humans alive, Dan Andriano. Andy's OK too. Credit: Brian Diaz.

Another smile? It's real! Brian Posehn and me at Disney, about to pitch a TV show that we ultimately sold . . . not to Disney.

Ruby and Zayda—two halves of my collective heart. I couldn't be prouder of these cuties.

When Ruby and I started that Irish stadium rock band in Joshua Tree.

Precious pumpkins plodding past poppies purposefully.

Ruby and Zayda acting like Trohmans. This was unprompted. I can't get enough of how fun they are.

When I'm not busy being ashamed of myself, I'm proudly displaying my beautiful children at places such as the mall, outside of establishments akin to, or exactly like, the Cheesecake Factory.

This was my best friend, Louie. He was my shadow. He knew me better than I knew myself. He will be sorely missed.

I liked to believe cowboy Louie enjoyed this hat. But if I were to engage with the truth, I'd come to realize it was his mortal enemy.

Say hi to Gary. He's all grade-A beef. But if this photo was a scratch-and-sniff, you'd pick up hints of fish piss and other types of urine.

now. We were lucky. We *are* lucky. That isn't to say we didn't work hard to get to where we are, but I wish I could have appreciated things back then, as I do today.

I don't want to give the impression that I ever felt I deserved anything the band had achieved. On the contrary, I never subscribed to the belief that any of what I have been so lucky to accomplish through the band is deserved, and I never will. But years and years ago, when Fall Out Boy began to grow larger than I could comprehend, it felt that this attained dream, of becoming this lead guitarist of a rock band, maybe wasn't all it was cracked up to be.

Suffice it to say, I wasn't happy with my new role in Fall Out Boy, whether it be on the creative front or live, where I felt like a fabulous dancing donkey, abusing his body onstage for the pleasure of gawking onlookers. I had envisioned that I'd be this man of stature, with a loud, ripping guitar, an extension of, or really a replacement for, my tiny, insignificant prick. Instead, everything at that moment felt nebulous. I was still defining myself by the band, but I did not know my own definition.

I took a lot of my frustration out on the guys. Not that I hit anyone or called them horrible names, but I was a black cloud through and through. I made sure that when they were around me, I would ooze such a sour mood that it would make them feel what I was feeling. That was beyond unfair. I regret that. I regret acting angry and petulant. My lack of self-esteem and confidence fed into a self-hatred that generated unnecessary turmoil. But this wasn't all about me; I know that. Relationships and dynamics within the band were getting mucky with or without my contributions to the filth. Drugs, unaddressed mental illness, and over-touring helped push us all to the brink of near destruction.

When we went to create the album that preceded our four-year break, *Folie à Deux*, I tried to reel myself back in. I showed up to preproduction; I was there every day in the studio. I don't think I had much to contribute to songwriting (I was still somewhat addled from substances), but I did my best to bring bits and pieces and riffs to the recording process. And I really tried to up my mood. It was somewhat fun making that album; I am proud of that one, despite the fact that the record label handled its release poorly.

Despite the somewhat-pleasant recording process, the damage was done within the band. When it came to touring the album, none of us wanted to share a space with one another or be stuck on the road, living that transient, nonscheduled, come-and-go-as-you-please lifestyle. And the fans revolted against *Folie*. We had middle fingers thrust toward our faces night after night. Bookending it all were copious backstage fights. What about? I can't totally recall. It was all fueled by burnout. We were burnt out on ourselves. And the world seemed burnt out on us. So we did what anyone would do when they feel not wanted: we went away.

Time apart from Fall Out Boy was needed. It gave me an opportunity to work with my new band, the heavier, less commercially dependent The Damned Things. I wrote the majority of the music for that first album, *Ironiclast*, which thrust me into a position of leadership, instilling a fair amount of self-confidence that I was able to bring back to Fall Out Boy, eventually. So nearly four years after announcing the famed hiatus, Fall Out Boy ushered in our return and made *Save Rock and Roll*. And this time, I brought music. Lots of it. I fought for things, in a communicative, healthy manner—free of anger and hard drugs. I did my best to be a part of the team and reassert myself. On top of that, I *tried* to stay positive. I had spent the prior four years not just working on my creative self but working on my mental health.

I did a re-up on my SSRI medication, got into regular therapy, and learned how to find an identity for myself that could exist on its own, outside of anything related to work—whether it be music or otherwise. I was intent on finding an inner peace of sorts, not necessarily in a traditionally Buddhist sense, but I wanted to know how I could be happy with me: Joe, the curly-haired, aloof, part–Mel/Albert Brooks, part–Jeff Spicoli guy in the corner. I learned that I felt lost because I lost myself, allowing my personality to be conflated with my band. I am not Fall Out Boy. And Fall Out Boy is certainly not me. Not by a long shot. And by fully realizing and coming to terms with that, I found some freedom.

When Fall Out Boy started making our eighth studio album, *Mania*, I did my best to assist, but that one sort of went off the rails for me. I feel that it's not our best effort, and I'm being kind. Don't get me wrong; there were some good ideas on there, and a song or two of worthwhile note. But in a way, it's a depiction of the band desperately searching for its own identity. I had become so content with me, with what I had going on, engrossed in making a second The Damned Things album and developing projects for television (not successfully, but having a ball trying), that I was OK with allowing everyone else to take that album in whatever direction it was to go in. I suppose I could've worked harder, yelled louder, fought, and done whatever else could have been done to make *Mania* turn out in a way I would've preferred, but I wasn't interested in the stress. I could see that if I thrust myself into that particular rat's nest, the old me, the black-cloud me, would come back out in full force. And I didn't need that. No one did.

Not everything can be a win. And that's OK. Some albums are good. Some are shit. Some art is art. Some art is trash, even if you thought it was a Monet sandwiched between a Pollock and a Renoir. And one must learn that, especially within a collaborative creative environment, you don't get to do everything. You must find your lane, what works for you and those around you. And in Fall Out Boy, I'm OK helping when I can, where I can, and getting out of the way when need be. Nineteen-year-old me would have retched at that idea, being a selfish, entitled blowhard who wanted to show the world how great he was. Well, you know what, teen me? Fuck you. You're the fucking worst. I'm glad I'm not you anymore. I've got a beard now and thick man skin. *Fear me.* Come get some, bitch! I'd kill you if you weren't already dead!

As I jot these thoughts down, I feel a sense of overwhelming serenity. I mean, who the hell gets to do what I do? I'm so lucky. I play guitar *for a job.* And I can support my family doing so. Plus, being able to bring happiness, in the form of song, to thousands of people a night, it feels like a public service. I'm not self-aggrandizing here; I realize people spend their hard-earned money to be served. But it's that exchange of energy, that life-affirming social experiment of playing live for a crowd, giving your all while they give the same back—what a wonderful thing.

For the first time in my short life, I can reflect upon my two-decade career in my band with pride: the good, the bad, the disgusting, and the abysmal. The embarrassing outfits. The unfathomable haircuts. The songs that have become classics for some. The ridiculous kissy-face photos for teen rags. The interviews where I completely let my guard down and talked about being a pathetic, spineless twerp. That time we played *SNL* and, instead of trying to sound good, thrashed around like morons. Those times we got to play Letterman a bunch. And that one time when Jay-Z introduced us onstage. That time I vomited inside our van, all over everyone, because I thought drinking an entire bottle of Bushmills was safe to do. I'm proud of it. All of it.

Except that awful cover of the original *Ghostbusters* theme. Sorry!

# Pills, Pills, Pills

The Oakwood Apartments in Toluca Hills, California, were situated on Barham Boulevard between the 101 Freeway and Warner Bros. Studios. I use the operative "was" because they've since renamed and rebooted the business to shed their lackluster and dated aesthetic. But it's still in the same location, and it probably serves the same purpose it always has. The Oakwoods were not your average apartments. They were, and maybe still are, used as temporary living spaces for people trying to make it in Hollywood. The oft-perused website Seeing-Stars.com claims that the likes of Michael C. Hall, Dean Stockwell, Neil Patrick Harris, and Aerosmith all had tenures at the Oakwoods. In my early twenties, when I stayed there not once but twice with Fall Out Boy to make our first two major-label albums, I did not see any other adults at the complex. From what I could tell, all the residents were children, carted around by their showbiz moms and dads, hoping to become the next Frankie Muniz or Amanda Bynes. There's an unsettling documentary, *The Hollywood Complex*, about the Oakwoods, following those lost souls; it's worth watching if you enjoy chasing your depression down a never-ending sewer hole of sadness, like I do. It took me about a week or so of living there to realize what a wretched vortex I had been sucked into.

I had been at the Oakwoods in 2004 with the rest of my band to make Fall Out Boy's major-label debut, *From Under the Cork Tree*, our breakthrough album that catapulted us from indie somewhat-darlings to tenuous mainstream starlets. Success is relative, and we were relatively certain that ours could be short-lived if we couldn't follow up with something bigger and better. This felt like a heavy burden, probably heavier on some than others. So in 2006, we returned to the Oakwoods. With the massive success of *From Under the Cork Tree*, one would assume we could afford to stay at fancier digs. But one element of Fall Out Boy's success is that we're very, very, very, *very* cheap. And so two years later we found ourselves once more at the gray, dismal, and isolated Oakwood Apartments complex on Barham.

My first go-around at the Oakwoods, and in Hollywood, was *incredibly* exciting. My standards weren't high, and I'd never experienced much hotel living outside of a Days Inn. This was a damn upgrade! I was just around twenty and had never been to Los Angeles, so that in itself was thrilling. And we were there to record a major-label album. Ho-ly shit! I had to let that sink in, often. At that point I was fortunate to have worked at one real-deal recording studio, back in the Midwest.

By 2004, when we bumped up to the big time, I don't think I was prepared for it in any way whatsoever. We went from making records for the hell of it to being in this contractually bound situation, running a single continuous session with a big, corporate budget in what felt like an exotic locale. I'd never been in a fancy LA studio, doing whatever it is I assumed fancy LA people do, which seemed way more upscale than whatever it was people did in the Midwest. We middle Americans drank Pabst and wore down jackets. The sun always shone in LA, and it felt *glorious*. It feels contrived to be inspired and propelled by the sun. Yet I allowed myself some optimism.

However, most of my time during that first stint in Los Angeles had little to do with being outside and catching those LA rays. I wasn't suntanning (my Ashkenazi skin can't handle it anyway), and I didn't walk any red carpets—I don't know why I would be allowed to or why I'd ever want to. I actually didn't know what I was supposed to do in LA. I spent most of that time inside a cavernous recording studio, being overwhelmed, feeling like a complete fraud, and trying to catch on to the new whatever the fuck was happening.

The band went from zero to a thousand in what felt like an overnight growth spurt and kept moving at that speed. As the baby in the band, I was just trying to keep up with the momentum. We were working with the biggest producer we'd worked with yet and facing the mounting pressure of expectations from Island Records, with their money on the line. It was scary. But that fear of failure on someone else's dime created a sense of excitement as well. Even though I would wake up every day crippled with nauseating fear that I was going to mess things up for everyone somehow simply by being there, at the end of the day I would go back to the Oakwoods feeling satisfied that I got to experience something new and be a part of something so much bigger than myself.

Roll tape to 2006, and we're back at the Oakwoods again. Only this time, I don't have that same wide-eyed fervor. I felt what road-worn band folk refer to as jaded, but truthfully, I wasn't apathetic; I was just severely dour. My good friend depression had come back in a big way. Not that "he" ever left ("he" never does), but at that time I was in a deeper state of self-loathing and dejection than normal. Fall Out Boy now existed within the high-octane world of the mainstream music industry. The band's newly established success had put some of the members in the forefront, deservedly so, and—as I've intimated—I found myself tucked neatly in the back, rather than shoulder to shoulder with the others. My perspective being what it is now, I think that's very normal. It's how bands must work to exist. Not everyone can be "the guy/gal." You need to understand your role in any environment and play to those strengths. But my role had changed in what felt like an instant. I had started Fall Out Boy five years prior, and to a large degree I co-led the charge. But when the stakes rose, I could not rise to the challenge.

I went from coleader to follower. That was devastating, to lose my hold, my footing, and suddenly feel like I had no idea how I fit in anymore. I was the guy who kept things together and moving forward, but that wasn't needed anymore—things were holding together just fine and moving quite well. Even if there was a problem to fix, that became a manager's job. I didn't have a guide to walk me through this process of finding my new place in the band. I felt useless. This wasn't anyone's fault but my own, keep in mind. I'm the master of my own emotions, my own domain; I was an adult, albeit a young one, and I could've done better to act like one. I'd been in therapy before, I knew it well as a helpful tool, and I could've gone back sooner, to gather new tools to help me sort through these issues and eventually find some autonomy, whether within or outside of the band, so I could feel whole again.

At the very least, I could've lost myself in recording this new album—sessions that would turn into our biggest album yet, *Infinity on High*. But those deep, dark, self-flagellating emotions made it nearly impossible for me to want to participate as much as I wish I had. The combination of mental illness and immaturity gave me the idea that I wasn't wanted, so therefore I should abscond. My impostor complex gave me intense anxiety on top of my heavy depression. I needed a way to quell it all, and quickly.

Around four years prior to making *Infinity on High*, Fall Out Boy had been touring Japan, still on our breakout album, *Take This to Your Grave*. Up until that tour, I'd followed a pretty strict Straight Edge lifestyle, an ideology that meant no drugs or alcohol usage. To some it also meant abstaining from sex, but I (a) didn't subscribe to that aspect of it and (b) wasn't getting laid anyway. I don't think I knew how to get laid. Being Straight Edge was a holdover from my time in the Chicago hardcore scene, but obviously it stems from a much deeper influence, established by older hardcore bands like DC's Minor Threat and NYC's Youth of Today.

So Fall Out Boy was in Tokyo, and I was nineteen. It was my first time in Japan, and if you haven't been to Tokyo, it's an intense place. With a population of over thirteen million people, and twice as many epilepsy-inducing neon signs, it feels intergalactic. Sofia Coppola's *Lost in Translation* does a fabulous job capturing not just the vivid and all-consuming aspects of the city—the frenetic lighting, the shoulder-to-shoulder buildings, the sea of people every which way—but also the city's loneliness. It's fascinating how you can feel so alienated in such a densely populated and lively place. I even noticed locals drinking and eating alone. Especially drinking. Other than one sneaky moment before Hebrew school when I snuck a couple of gulps of a neighbor kid's parent's rum and became slightly tipsy, I'd never been drunk.

At that time in Fall Out Boy's career, we were just beginning to travel internationally. I, more than the rest of the guys, would walk about on my own in each city. On one of our first tours of the UK, I would wake up early to explore every town and village, trying to find UK and European editions of albums from the Manchester scene to fill out my growing collection. But buying records or not, I always wanted to explore, and I liked doing it solo. And so here we were in Tokyo, and I was walking around on my own, late at night, and everyone was drinking. It looked fun. The legal age to drink in Japan is twenty, but I had been told it was nineteen. Drinking is a big part of Japanese culture, and I gather they don't seem to take the legal age limit very seriously there, or perhaps it was difficult to read the exact age on my white-guy face.

Seeing the nightlife come alive in tandem with alcohol made me question my relationship with Straight Edge. I was afraid to "break it," as the phrase goes, worried that my bandmates (who were also Straight Edge at the time) would disown me. I worried some of my Straight Edge friends would stop talking to me. As stupid as that sounds, and it was stupid, relationships became ruined over people "breaking Edge" in the hardcore scene. But goddammit, man, I didn't understand why I had to limit myself anymore. I wanted to have a jolly good time. So an underage Jew walked into a bar and sat down at the counter, and the bartender didn't tell him to leave. Score! Now I just had to figure out how to order my first-ever alcoholic drink in a foreign country where I did not know how to speak Japanese. Piece of cake. With no Google Translate or tiny English-to-Japanese book, I just held out my hand as if I were holding a phantom glass and mimed drinking. The bartender looked at me kindly, then poured me a whiskey.

It was the perfect amount, about two or three fingers. Now, whiskey is a sippin' drink, but at the time I was not in the know of many things, or anything. So I slammed the whole glass in a hurried gulp, and boy, did it *burn*. As I retched and nervously reached into my pocket to pay the good man, a move that took me thirty anxious seconds, I suddenly felt a warm rush emanate through my body—and it felt . . . nice. M'lord, I'd never felt so good! I was just a twig of a man; the booze hit me like a Mack truck. I then slapped far too much money on the counter, as payment, and stumbled out of the bar— instantaneously plastered. Soon after, the bartender hurriedly ran out after me.

I had no knowledge of Japanese rules and customs, and I was afraid the bartender had discovered I was underage, some- how. I didn't know what was going to happen; I just thought I was in trouble. My constant fear again: getting in trouble. But the bartender wasn't out for me; he just gave me some change. It turns out tips are not customary in Japan.

"Thank you, myyyy *favorite* man!" I slurred as I threw the money in the air like Scrooge McDuck upon feeling the Christmas spirit of it all.

I then proceeded to sprint down the street, yelling nothing comprehensible while I continued to re-up, drinking all night, and every night subsequently on that tour. One eve- ning I drank nothing but beach rum drinks, did karaoke alone, sang a lot of new wave hits, and was propositioned by a prostitute to "make it as big as a balloon." As she mimed an air blow job, I politely declined. The idea of my penis becom- ing so erect that it would turn comically large, round, and beet red sounded painful. Man, I had a lot of fun on that trip. Yet the overall experience, as positive as it felt at the time, is what led me down a path of secretively putting things in my body to feel good all the time so I wouldn't feel bad any of the time at all.

When using drugs and alcohol to ward off your problems, you'll find you must keep taking stronger drugs and drinking more and more to push said problems away. Your tolerance will build, and your problems will keep following you. They want to be dealt with. They won't be ignored. And here I was, face-to-face with my depression, my anxiety, and my feelings of complete and utter insecurity and incompetence within my band, which at the time was my entire life. It felt awful, and I didn't want to feel it. I didn't want to feel like the failure in the middle of a success sandwich. I didn't want to face my problems. I didn't even really understand, clearly, what the root of my problems was at the time.

In 2006, I stood in the bathroom of my temporary living situation at the Oakwoods and took a swig of liquid codeine that I had procured earlier that week from a very lenient "rock doc." That's the pet name we give to doctors who adore people in bands and wish they could've been in bands themselves. Some of them even play in bar bands to live out their fantasies for a moment. Mine was a lap-steel player. Rock docs ingratiate themselves with real band folk just to feel the aura of rock stardom. I don't believe that aura exists. At least it doesn't exist in me. For whomever it does "exist," it's probably just extreme narcissism. But rock docs love whatever "it" is, and they'll trade you a prescription for some basking. As I stared at my sorry self in the mirror, it was clear to me that the codeine wasn't doing it.

Unlike my stint making *Cork Tree*, when I was isolated in the studio, working, not socializing, this go-around I had friends in Los Angeles—Chaz and Rylie. Rather than spend time working on this new album, I'd spend time with them. They lived close to Paramount Studios in Hollywood proper and would have me over during the day to get stoned and talk about whatever it is stoned twentysomething idiots talked about. Eating? Smoking more weed?

Getting stoned can be great. Weed can be great. As a reluctant adult who has found his center and kicked all his nasty drinking and drug habits, I still smoke pot, occasionally. But I only do this at night when my kids are in bed. For me, it's a way to wind down, space out, and crash on the couch after a long day of thinking and working and rearing small humans. It's not an all-encompassing, world-devouring coping mechanism.

When you're in your early twenties, working through intense emotional issues, weed is not a good fix. It's not the right type of medicine for handling problems as large as the ones I had. I could tell the cannabis wasn't doing it. I'd smoke some with Chaz and Rylie, and it would take the edge off, but the high would wear off too, and I'd be back to high anxiety. I'd then cycle through that, over and over, living in a haze of green smoke. As I discovered that weed wasn't strong enough to mask my darkest emotions, I came to the conclusion that I wanted to go deeper and take harder drugs, to "fully eliminate" my problems.

One day, when I was in the midst of elaborating on my woes to my friends, one of them handed me a pill. I was already so high, and too young to understand the concept of mortality, that I took it without caring what *it* was. Before the threats of prostate exams and high cholesterol entered my everyday lexicon, I thought I was invincible. In the early 2000s, I didn't have the understanding I do today regarding narcotic pills; there hadn't been wide news coverage of the opioid crisis. The danger in using wasn't discussed in my school the same way that alcohol, weed, and other "hard" drugs had been. And because seemingly harmless over-the-counter medicine came in pill form, the pills themselves seemed innocuous—plus, they didn't have to be smoked or injected into a vein. Considering my past experience with things such as food, swallowing crap seemed like a pain-free, no-risk, all-reward endeavor.

The pill in question was OxyContin. And when it kicked in, I was more or less on the floor for the rest of the day. That first high, it was amazing. I was up, but I'd never been so down at the same time. I kept trying to climb upward to escape my depression, anxiety, and self-hatred. If I had known that the best way to avoid dealing with my emotional state was to duck deep down beneath the surface of reality through pill-form heroin, I would've probably been eating handfuls years earlier. I probably would've been dead.

Soon after, I obviously wanted more. Unlucky for me, Chaz and Rylie's drug dealer, K., was *literally* across the street. K. lived in a house with a couple of derelicts who seemed to pose no threat. On even the sunniest of days, K.'s house was dark, littered with the token dealer accoutrements—scales, pipes, stacks of cash, etc. He was a nice guy, all in all, not the stereotypical scary, hard-edged dealer you might find within the likes of a hard-boiled Dennis Lehane novel. He was bubbly, was constantly stoned, and had *all* the pills.

I started buying Oxy from K. but eventually took on Adderall to balance out the sluggish effects of the opioid. Eventually I would start buying pill-form morphine to help with my chronic back pain. K. had it all. I used to take each of these pills to counteract the others, but sometimes I'd take them all at once. I remember the amalgam effect being somewhere between a long-form whippet and an LSD trip. Sometimes I'd end up vomiting. Other times I'd just pass out and be fortunate to wake back up. As irresponsible as that all was, I would often wash these fine medications down with a case of light beer—my body dysmorphia dictated that I count calories!

I spent the next six years addicted to pills. I eventually ditched the Adderall and morphine, opting to stick to Oxy or hydrocodone—one and the same, to a degree. When I moved to Manhattan a couple of years later, I often lazed around in my 680-square-foot apartment in the Village, upside down on the couch, my entire body tingling from the effects of the drug, laughing and drooling like a slob.

It's odd and disconcerting to admit that I spent two of Fall Out Boy's early major-label record cycles completely out of my mind. It's disappointing. I know I had a lot of unresolved issues and a remarkable amount of self-hatred that I did not want to confront. The band itself was a ticking time bomb as well—we were making music and touring to such an intense extent that we, as human beings, were breaking down from the stress and lack of grounding in our lives. I wasn't the only one using substances to cope, nor was I the only one with demons. We, as a band, had been pushed too hard for too long.

Four years into my addiction, Fall Out Boy went on our infamous four-year hiatus. Some people say we broke up. Sure. Whatever. Tack on whatever descriptor you need to tack on; we needed time apart from the big machine that engulfed the band, the forced workaholism that would've driven us to an actual breakup if we hadn't intervened ourselves. In addition, I really needed to find myself outside of the band, as I was still trying to understand and grasp my identity and role in the world.

Before Fall Out Boy went on this break, I had started the inklings of a side project with Scott Ian, of Anthrax fame.

That project became The Damned Things, a band that also comprised Keith Buckley of the late Every Time I Die and my Fall Out Boy bandmate Andy Hurley. It was an incredible sense of validation to have Scott, someone I looked up to as a music hero, put his trust in the "other guy" from Fall Out Boy to drive the engine of his new band. Just as I am very proud of my history with Fall Out Boy, I'm incredibly proud of what we have done with The Damned Things. It gave me a renewed sense of purpose at a time when I was flailing, looking for something to grab on to. But unfortunately, when it came to my pill habit, I was in too deep to get out on my own.

After making the first The Damned Things album, *Ironiclast*, we went on numerous tours, and I developed a cocaine habit as well. The cocaine never got as bad as the pills—it took way too much of an effort to get, and pills were cheaper and easier to come by. I confined the new habit to the road for a while, but eventually it too came back with me to cozy up to the pills and booze in my own home. After an abrupt finish to the *Ironiclast* touring cycle, due to Hurricane Irene's ravaging of the Southeast, I absconded back to New York and floundered around some more, dipping my toes into different musical projects to no real avail—a three-piece noise rock band, With Knives, and a half-hearted stretch making music for ad agencies.

Eventually we got the band back together, when Patrick and I spent three hours on the phone discussing what we missed about each other, in a musical sense. That was nice. It got me excited about Fall Out Boy again, and I felt like I was discovering a potential new role within the band. I also felt more content than before taking a back seat. Doing The Damned Things helped with that, but so did age and perspective. While I returned to my alma mater with a newer and healthier exterior view, I did not return with a healthy interior. I was dope sick. And it took a worlds-collide scenario to bring my illness to the forefront.

When Fall Out Boy did some theater-sized gigs in London to promote our comeback, Scott Ian happened to be in town as well, and he came out to one of the shows. It was wonderful to see him, and I was anxiously awaiting his feedback on our set. Before he showed up to the venue, I did what I had been doing for years to prepare for the show: I ate a grip of Oxy. I didn't even count the pills. We were an hour from stage time when Scott arrived to say hello. To my surprise though, he skipped the formalities altogether and went right to the core.

"You look green," Scott bluntly told me.

Scott has been around the block. He's seen a lot of his friends make bad decisions, and I believe he knew exactly what was happening as soon as he saw me. I don't remember what I said in response. I know that I ran to the dressing room, under the guise of needing to get ready, and began to examine my face in the bathroom mirror. Scott was wrong; I wasn't green—I was also yellow. And I had dark bags under my eyes. Not the types of bags that you get from one bad night's sleep. Not even the kind you get from staying up all night with a newborn. These bags looked like little beaver tails. Not the cute kind. These were disgusting. I was disgusting. I was covered in a thin film of sweat. I had a sheen. There were plenty of moments over the course of my six-year struggle when I could have noticed this, and I never seemed to care until someone I respected, and who respected me enough to be honest with me, told me the cold, hard truth. Scott's colorful diagnosis was all I needed—to know that I was a junkie.

I quit pills that day.

I've seen it many times over, loved ones who have succumbed to their own addictions. Some of my closest friends died from mainlining heroin. People in my family have fallen ill with their diseases and gone to recovery. It's easy to look down at people for their addictions, to shame them, to say, "I'm better than that." It's just as easy to point the finger as it is to become addicted yourself, especially since we live in a world that doesn't offer proper mental health services and normalizes addictive tendencies with your local Bed Bath & Beyond selling "It's wine o'clock somewhere!" wooden plaques to every Middle American housewife looking for that funky piece for the kitchenette.

As somebody who has seen the depths and works hard every day to stay clean, I am grateful. Grateful to be alive. Grateful to be there for my kids. I'm also grateful to have had all these experiences to learn from. Like the time I smoked crack! I really did. But more on that in the tenth-anniversary gilded-edition bonus chapter of this book: "My Neck, My Back, I'm No Pussy, I Smoked Crack!"

# Those Darn Things

Creating to fruition is a remarkable feat. Manifesting something from nothing, taking an abstract concept, then removing it from abstraction to deliver it into tangible reality—it's a truly impressive exploit, no matter who you are. However, given my uncouth nature, I liken creating to shitting; I make the shit in my body and desperately need to get that shit out, no matter what. And it feels lovely to release that shit, but once that shit is out, I do not need to reference that shit anymore, as it is stinky, gross shit. I am now ready to move forward, on to making more shit. But it's not that I don't love the shit I've made or been a part of creating. It's more that I'm the type of person who cannot stop making things and will never be satisfied with just one creation, or two, or twenty. Like the old shark myth, I need to keep swimming, or I shall surely perish. Or in terms of shitting, if I let my shit fester, I'll die of creative sepsis.

But what about when you create something that doesn't fill you with pride? From my experience, you'll do whatever it takes not just to obfuscate that abomination but to burn its existence to the ground, no matter the earth scorched. It's paramount for the ego to eliminate any embarrassment and shame posthaste to save yourself and what little dignity remains. That goes twofold for anyone living and working in the public sphere, as the idea of outside ridicule, attached to something so privately terrible, is genuinely a sickening feeling. Hence, you cannot watch Jerry Lewis's *The Day the Clown Cried*, or on a less Holocaust-y but still terrible tangent, purchase an in-print copy of Fall Out Boy's "first album," *Evening Out with Your Girlfriend*.

I recently came across an online article, from Britain's *Rock Sound* magazine, with the accompanying headline, "It's Time We Give 'Fall Out Boy's Evening Out with Your Girlfriend' the Respect It Deserves." Now, I truly mean no disrespect to the writer, or the publication, who has always held us in good standing, and I them. But that record, if you choose to call it one, does not deserve anyone's respect. While it does exist, and I suppose it deserves its place in time and space, it is not good. It's beyond not good. This album should only exist as a histor-ical reference point to understand how bad one's band can be before it gets *less* bad. Listening to that album is like watching someone have their first-ever sexual experience: it's going to look unfortunate, be very messy, probably be a bit painful for some, and be all-around confusing. First sex is terrible sex, and this first record is *Terrible Sex: The Musical*. And yet, with *Eve-ning Out*, people still want to hold it in some sort of regard that isn't warranted—hence articles being written about it eighteen years later. *The Rolling Stone Album Guide* even awarded it two stars, which is generous. They should have created a new rating system replacing the stars with images of explosive diarrhea and awarded it five out of five burning-hot sloppy ones.

Fast-forward six years later, to 2009, with three respectable studio albums under our belt; Fall Out Boy releases *Folie à Deux*. By far, this was our most ambitious album, something that pushed our musical boundaries and pried open space within the genre for similar artists to experiment with more than just aping other pop-punk acts. While we had been thoughtfully establishing change from album to album, by the time *Folie* hit, we were less narrowly defined. We weren't a pop-punk or emo band. To me, it felt as if this was our version of Queen's shift from the hard rock of *Sheer Heart Attack* to the genre-bending experimentation of *A Night at the Opera*. No one else seemed to feel that way.

While it was fun creating *Folie* in the studio, the reaction from fans, more than critics, really took the wind out of our sails. But even before our fans took it to task, the label botched the release strategy. Island had decided to release our first single, "I Don't Care," a little over two months ahead of the album release itself. And while the single proved successful (going platinum, receiving tons of airplay, and even making it onto *Rolling Stone*'s Best 100 Songs of 2008), releasing the song so far out from the album made it hard for people to make the connection that the song was a precursor to the album. So when *Folie* was released, people had no clue that it was the same album that included the hit single "I Don't Care." And so the result of this poor marketing decision was poor album sales. We went from selling records in the millions to barely cracking gold with this one.

We got to experience the poor fan reaction in less of an online way and more of an in-your-face way. At many of our live shows, concertgoers made it their mission to get to the show early so they could stand at the front of the barricade and flick us off for the entire set. Before *Folie*, we were like Slayer to these kids; they wouldn't fuck with anything except Fall Out Boy. Now they were telling Fall Out Boy to go fuck itself.

Stacking atop this humiliation was the fact that, from 2001 to 2009, we had never really had a break of any kind—no time at home to decompress and plant roots. Part of what got Fall Out Boy to where we were, at that moment, was the relentless touring and album crafting. And after eight years of going at it, never stopping, being on the road for over two hundred days a year, the cracks were starting to show. But my cracks had been showing for far longer. And by this point, I was so deep in the forest of it all that I could not see, or fully appreciate, being in a hugely successful rock band with an exceptional career—recent low album sales and literal fuck-yous aside.

Imagine starting a career at seventeen, and it just takes off. Then you're working alongside the same people, day in and day out, practically living with them, rarely going home, and rarely taking a real pause. And you've started this as a teenager, so you're growing up in front of strangers. You get lost in the work and the gears of the industry itself. The job then becomes more about interviews, photoshoots, and sales than it ever is about the music. Then you wake up one day and realize you're not entirely sure who you are, independent of that position or those people. I couldn't separate myself from the band, and I desperately wanted to know who Joe was, which drove me crazy. You'd go mad too. You'd lose sight of not just the incredible gift in front of your face but everything around you because you never had it to begin with. Everyone needs a moment to come up for air; otherwise, the lack of oxygen to the noggin will make smart brain go dum-dum.

Around the time the *Folie à Deux* album cycle imploded, I was about twenty-four and still holding on to a lot of confused, negative emotions, feeling like both an interloper in my own band and a fraud as a musician; intense impostor syndrome is another talent of mine that I still wear unabashedly on my sleeve to this day. More on that later! Anyway, up until that moment, I had been adrift, unsure of what my role was, not just in Fall Out Boy but in my own life. I felt as if I had been on this breakneck roller-coaster ride for years, blindfolded, unable to see where I was headed, just letting the open car take me wherever it pleased. But I desperately wanted off the ride, for at least a moment, so I could take off the blindfold and see what was happening around me. And maybe I'd find a new ride to try out—something my speed.

A year or so prior to the *Folie* fallout, I had been introduced to Scott Ian from Anthrax, through a mutual friend, David Karon. This happened at a fancy Italian restaurant in West Hollywood, and I was nervous as all hell. Until then, I had made it a point in my career to never meet my heroes; I wasn't in the business of killing my idols. I'd rather let them exist far away from me as phantoms. I once had a chance to meet Morrissey, someone whose lyrics I have tattooed not once but twice on my bod. But I politely declined and am still glad to this day I never took the offer, especially considering his awful takes as of late. A real shame about those tattoos.

However, I trust David, he's never led me astray, and so I gave in to his goading to join him and Scott for dinner. David's more laid-back than myself, but we're both huge dorks, and I figured if Scott liked David's dorkitude, perhaps he would, at the very least, tolerate mine. I also made it a point, internally, to make sure *not* to express my Anthrax fandom, whatsoever. "Play it cool, Joe," I'd recite to myself aloud in the shower, and the car, and under my breath outside of the car, and most definitely in my head once inside the fancy-schmancy Italiano joint.

Once I arrived at Osteria Mozza, I came to a large, round table where, among some unknowns, David sat next to Scott

Ian, with his signature goatee and stoic facial expression that seemed to say, in a heavy Queens accent, "It's *your* funeral, pal." Yet the moment I sat down, Scott's face softened, and he immediately addressed my existence. I could've just gotten up right then, taken a cab home, and felt like the night was a big success! But we quickly started talking about stuff we both like, which is a thing band guys tend to do to suss out who is in our tribe. I don't mean the Jewish tribe, which we both are most definitely in. I mean the nerdish tribe. And the nerdy stuff I like happens to be the nerdy stuff Scott likes—comic books, horror movies, skateboarding, metal (duh), guitars (durr). But the coup de grâce that solidified our new best friendship was our mutual love for Ireland's greatest band *of all time*, Thin fucking Lizzy.

Now, a lot of people might be surprised to learn that Thin Lizzy is a big influence on Fall Out Boy; Patrick and I used to do a pretty decent rendition of "The Boys Are Back in Town." I'll even brag a little about the time Fall Out Boy rehearsed next to the reformed Thin Lizzy, which entailed some classic members, such as Scott Gorham. We could hear them playing the hits next door—"Jailbreak" and "Cowboy Song," among others—which got us thoroughly excited. And then we ran through what we needed to rehearse for, whatever that was— and it sure felt low-rent in comparison. But then, as suddenly as we finished, John Sykes, who also played in motherfucking Whitesnake, popped in—nearly a foot taller than us all and, even in his old age, ten feet cooler looking than any of us, with his beautiful blond shoulder-length locks. And Sykes, nicer than nice could be, went on and on about how much he liked our band, our pop sensibility, and how that's kind of what Thin Lizzy was built around—hooks, hooks, and more hooks. Any- time I feel like I don't belong in the rock world, I remember that moment, and it makes me feel 3–5 percent less like a big, fat faker.

Thin Lizzy is a great equalizer, as they were for Scott and me. Our love for that band, for old-fashioned, catchy rock 'n' roll with a bit of grit, is what prompted us to start what would eventually become a band of its own. So while Fall Out Boy was crafting and subsequently touring on *Folie à Deux*, Scott and I would meet any time I was in LA and craft our own songs. Eventually I whispered to Andy, the other metalhead in Fall Out Boy, "Hey, come play drums for this thing I'm doing with Scott fucking Ian!" He didn't say no. So now we had a great drummer. Then Scott and I gabbed about how much we love the band Every Time I Die, and I reached out to their singer, one of my closest friends, Keith Buckley, and voilà! Now we had a singer. And now we had a band—a straight-up, dirty, soon-to-be-catchy rock band. Like the early Fall Out Boy days, I was weirdly back to driving the ship once more. And Scott Ian, a true legend, was trusting me for some reason. But this time around, I knew how to hold on to the wheel, or at least help to keep us from running off the road.

I had this new group, and I was excited about it—it wasn't totally real yet, but it felt close, and we were having so much fun in the honeymoon phase of it all. But while that was going on, I was still on tour, getting flicked off every night. And I was with a bunch of guys that I now couldn't stand being around because we were never *not* around or on top of each other. I was just done with the whole kit and caboodle: the band, the press circus, the angry fans, and the never-ending cycle of "make a record, tour, make a record, tour, make a record, tour" without any real breaks. Again, I was on this ride and had no control over it.

I wasn't the only one feeling the weight as things began to cave in. Patrick and I were both ready to have some time at home and tackle new endeavors—he had been jonesing to make a solo album, which I wanted to hear. Andy, the most go-with-the-flow, game-for-anything kind of guy in the band, probably would've been OK with continuing, but I wanted him to come play drums with Scott, Keith, and me. Pete, on the other hand, wasn't ready to give up, but I could see how the grind was wearing on him too.

We kicked and screamed our way through the rest of the *Folie* tour, getting into a shouting match somewhere in Australia, where I "gracefully" stomped out of the room when I got too heated because . . . *ta-da*! I was horrible at confrontation! I'm only 50 percent better at nearly forty years old, so hopefully by eighty I'll master the concept. Near the end of the run, we had a more civil roundtable discussion back in Chicago— much calmer, no screaming—with our manager to help guide us to a conclusion. This is where we more or less decided to take that indefinite break, the reviled hiatus. I don't exactly remember how it was framed, but everyone aired their grievances the best they could—which at that time was equivalent to grunting like a gaggle of partially evolved man-chimps— and once the tour was over, it was just over. Not broken-up over, just not happening. We publicly uttered the word "hiatus," which can mean putting on ice, taking a pause, a momentary delay, a gap in the series. But people, especially fans, heard "breakup." It started with Andy tweeting the word "hiatus," which probably wasn't the best method of delivering the news. Pete then had to explain the definition of the word "hiatus" in interviews, which didn't seem to calm any fears. It probably didn't help that Pete also blogged and tweeted various thoughts about being both uncertain and dismal about the band's future. He wasn't wrong, though; things were uncertain, and the way we left things felt somewhat dismal.

Fall Out Boy, at the end of the day, is driven by Pete. And I think he had gotten so used to driving, pedal to the metal, that when we abruptly threw on the parking brake, it shook him. We never had a proper conversation about taking a healthy break for *x* amount of time, then returning to Fall Out Boy, refreshed, which would've injected some optimism into the situation. Yes, we talked clearly about taking a break, but our future was left open-ended. It had been clear, for years, that we were a collective emotional mess with severe communication issues, which needed some real massaging if we were ever to get back to it.

I remember attempting to elaborate on this in an email to Pete in which I suggested pulling an idiotic *Some Kind of Monster* group therapy session with a mediator and figuring out how to unravel our tangled mess. I mean, it's not a bad idea on its own, but I was in no place to tell anyone to go to therapy, since I had needed it for a while myself. Needless to say, this fell on deaf ears, as it should've. I don't blame him for not wanting to hear any of it; the wounds were too fresh, and everyone needed space from the situation, and from each other.

I sent that very stupid email from a mentally fragile place but also from a physically real place called Montana Studios. Montana Studios is not in Montana. It is also not in North Dakota, South Dakota, Idaho, or Wyoming. It does not exist within US mountain time or upon the Great Plains. No, the Montana Studios sit at Eleventh Avenue between Fifty-Sixth and Fifty-Seventh Street in Manhattan. Since I was living in New York at the time, Keith was in Buffalo, and Scott was often in the city, The Damned Things congregated there for rehearsal.

That was what we named the band, The Damned Things—a fluid Keith Buckley idea that hit all the right notes. In my failure to allay Pete's hopelessness regarding Fall Out Boy's future, all I could do was shrug and focus on getting ready to tour with my new band. Oh, *and* we still had to make a record.

Almost instantly after Fall Out Boy hit the brakes, I jumped from one coaster to the next, getting The Damned Things' debut record, *Ironiclast*, ready for public consumption. Due to my recording contract with Island, we were forced to release the album through them, which came with some perks, mainly a nice budget—which we quickly squandered. Whatever didn't go to the actual recording itself seemed to go to our ex-guitarist Rob Caggiano's daily sushi habit. I doubt we were the reason why folks in big bands don't receive big recording budgets for their side projects anymore, but I feel like we were one of the last and may have contributed more than a drop to that toxic bucket.

Being on a major label, we also got to track the album at top-notch studios. We did the drums at Hendrix's legendary Electric Lady Studios, straight to tape, then did the remainder at a beautiful spot in a Brooklyn warehouse with windows in the control room that displayed a nearly 360-degree view of Manhattan and Williamsburg. We had a lot of fun making that record and wasting all the money on high-end takeout.

Despite the money squandered, when we finished the record, we had made something that I believe had substance—real guitar-driven songs, with great lyrics, catchy hooks, and a ridiculous number of guitar solos. While there was the fear on my end that this album might sound dated, considering it was 2010 and the pop-music world was shying away from bands with intentional guitar solos, or guitar at all, we managed to keep one foot in the yesteryear with another firmly planted in the now. We set out to make the album Scott and I had talked about, our ode to Thin Lizzy, but modern and all our own. I was proud.

Now that we had the record, and I was listening to it *and* pleased with it, and I was staring at the artwork, and it looked good, I was suddenly overcome with a stark realization: we had to share it with people. This notion sent me into a spiral of crippling anxiety. The worst part about creating is deciding whether you should share your creation. You're not just opening yourself up to feedback; you're opening yourself up to critique. Like my friend Josh Newton had said, sharing your art is opening your legs to show people your tiny dick, or blown-out vagina, or whatever element of your nudity disgusts you most. And there's an excellent chance people will laugh, or jeer, or jeer with laughter.

So there I was, dick in hand, and I realized I had no choice; I had to wag it at people. A major record label, who would not promote this thing, still paid us to make an album, and there was an expectation that we would release the material they owned in the hopes that *maybe* they'd make some of their money back. We were set to drop our first single, "We've Got a Situation Here," along with a hilarious *Ghostbusters*-meets-superhero-origin-story music video, directed by one of my close friends, the ever-talented Brendon Small. I adored these things we were about to put out to the world, but I assure you I could not breathe the morning of the drop.

Up to that moment, I was mostly known to the world for having the big hair that non-Jews would refer to as my "Jew-fro" (a microaggression that I often let slide), and being a stoner (what?), and, um . . . that's it, I think? I didn't want those things to be my legacy, but I also didn't want to add "responsible for a terrible, horrible, no-good, garbage, cum-dumpster side project" to that list. However, I couldn't do anything to stop the impending doom as the music left its cozy, secret hidey-hole and ventured out to be castrated by the court of public opinion.

As the songs went live, I writhed in controlled terror as I quickly refreshed various websites to revel in the negative feedback—I just wanted it over with. I refreshed again. And again. And one more time. Then I realized something: people need a moment to hear a song before they can hate the song. So I set a timer on my phone for four and one-half minutes, roughly the length of the song itself, and waited. After the alarm, I refreshed every music website I had opened, once again. And again. Then I waited five seconds. Then more refreshing. Then finally . . . results.

I could see comments pouring in, and I instinctively shut my eyes, out of fear, then slowly opened them, as if taking in the barbs by itsy-bitsy degrees would ease the blows. But once I fully opened my peepers, I was taken aback—people liked the song. And they thought the video was funny; it was not my doing, but still, great to be associated with someone else's good work. At the end of the day, I pulled the same shitheel move that I continue to practice to this day: I work myself up, one heart attack away from a stroke about a scenario that is out of my control, but then everything turns out A-OK. Sure, maybe I'll die young from stress, but I'm *not* leaving a beautiful corpse. You can't make me!

When all was said and done, the album got reviewed well and even charted number one on *Billboard*'s Heatseekers. Sure, there was the occasional hate review or comment such as "Nothing special," "Fuck these guys," and "I wish the two guys from Fall Out Boy would die in a nuclear holocaust that only killed them and no one else." Of course, my fragile baby ego read every one of those negative comments and used them as additional depression fodder. But the news was in, and the record was one of merit to most people. I felt good about that, for about five minutes. Oh, depression.

Not long after the release of *Ironiclast*, before we embarked on promoting the album, my wife, Marie, and I headed out to Los Angeles. We were to meet Scott, his wife, and a group of other "total rockers" to party in the New Year and celebrate Scott's birthday. It was a happy, carefree moment in my life; I had accomplished a herculean task, making a record without Fall Out Boy that people didn't hate. The fear of rejection had passed, and I could unwind, a novel concept for me. So, of course, to achieve max relax, I sniffed and snorted large amounts of white powder up my nose, a classic way to take. It. Easy.

As my body jittered around the room like a Hunter S. Thompson caricature, everyone started doing that thing they do on New Year's Eve, where they count backward from ten *really* loud—I always forget about that part. It terrifies me. As quick on my feet as I was, the holes in my cocaine brain took a minute to register that we were seconds away from ringing in the New Year. And of course, like I did most years, after everyone yells, "One!" and kisses each other, I picked up my phone and called my parents. The phone rang, and I rubbed my fingers across my teeth and numb gums, an all-American boy hyped up on the all–South American drug. My mom picked up the phone.

"Hello?"

"Happy New Year, Mom!" I screamed.

"Oh, hi! You know what, I've been meaning to talk to you," she replied, something clearly on her mind.

"What's that?" I happily said, *way* too high to realize there was a venomous snake's head on the other end of the rattle.

"Well, your father played me that new record you made . . ."

"Oh yeah? Whaddya think?" I was such a coked-up idiot.

"Well, I liked everything there, except what *you* did."

And *there* was the rejection.

# I Fret, Therefore I Am

Wat is a guitar? *Merriam-Webster* defines the instrument as follows:

gui·tar | \ gə-ˈtär:

*A longish woody hard thing with a bunch of stuff in it. It also has other stuff on the outside. Plus, it has these weird lines. But the weird lines aren't ordinary weird lines. Don't be fooled! These "lines" are little metal danger ropes. They will hurt your soft fingers. 'Cause they're made of metal, remember—just like cars and frying pans and also refrigerators too. However, if you can figure out how to touch those metal ropes and not yell "Ouch!" and get past the blisters on your fingers after you fiddle on the ouch ropes, you can make the instrument sound all like, "Diddly-doo a-twang-a-dee, flip-flap-ding-a-twerp, whip-i-dee-whee!" And then, if you get really good at it, and it's also still the 1980s, you'll get a blow job!*

But I believe the instrument is far more multidimensional than that.

I discovered the guitar as a young lad in the 1990s. I'll set the scene: President George "Contra Shmantra" Bush was nearing the end of his reign. The only thing Ryan Gosling was driving was tweens, wild with early-onset horniness, on the set of *The Mickey Mouse Club*. Everyone was forced to own a Game Boy, lest they be executed, on-site within their local McDonald's smoking section. MTV was still just a music video television network that played, primarily, music videos. And many of these music videos were produced by rock bands, rife with guitars. I was about seven or eight back then.

At the time, popular music felt more varied than today. There was something on the radio for everyone. If you wanted straight-up pop, you had Ace of Base and New Kids on the Block. Hip-hop was on this new level, hitting an insane stride, from Nas and Wu-Tang Clan on the East Coast to Dr. Dre's *The Chronic* pushing West Coast hip-hop into the cultural zeitgeist. And let's not forget the thumping booty worship of Sir Mix-a-Lot, making those of us on the whiter side of life ponder the backsides that we had ignored for *far* too long. We had ethereal dreamscapes from the likes of trip-hop wizards Portishead. There were the heroin-hued industrial sounds of Nine Inch Nails. And singer-songwriters like PJ Harvey and Alanis Morissette made us look a little more inward. You oughta know!

I was firmly attracted to the loud and guitar-driven acts such as Nirvana, the Pixies, Pearl Jam, the Smashing Pumpkins, the Breeders, Alice in Chains, Pantera, Weezer, and Oasis. The real list actually goes on and on, and on and on. There was no shortage of noisy guitar bands. And I love it all. I say "love" because those artists, and that decade, it's still my bread and butter. Even though I am currently listening to Ol' Dirty Bastard's "Hippa to da Hoppa," the next song on my playlist is most definitely Soundgarden's "Rusty Cage," a song that includes the heaviest breakdown known to both the natural and unnatural world.

In 1991, Guns N' Roses put out the spotty *Use Your Illusion* albums. Warts and all pending, I distinctly remember watching the music video for "November Rain" from *Illusion I*. And whatever anyone wants to say about that album, or every unfortunate release from the band since, that song has not one but two of the greatest guitar solos known to humankind. The song itself is fantastic, but if you were to remove the solos from the song, allowing them to be played disembodied, they'd sing like two classical arias, meant to elicit full-body goose bumps. And I can safely assume that, if and when advanced alien lifeforms arrive on Earth to enslave us all, they will force Slash into rockin' indentured servitude to perform those two solos ad nauseam until he crumbles into a fine pile of organic dust, leaving behind only a leathery top hat and a flame-topped Les Paul.

In elementary school, watching this Slash guy play solo one of two, in front of an abandoned church in the desert, awoke a dormant part of me, one that yearned to be cool. Right then and there, at age nine, I discovered what a childhood dream was. Most kids around me, at that time, wanted only the basics—to become firefighters, veterinarians, astronauts, or race car drivers. But I wanted to be Slash. I was determined to be a very hip-looking, very stylish, iconic lead guitar player. (I did not achieve the hip or stylish or iconic aspects of that dream, but one out of four is still 25 percent!)

I have previously detailed that, up until wrapping my mitts around the guitar, I had been put through a ringer of far less sexy instruments: creepy cat piano lady, viola (the violin's unattractive cousin), and, of course, the ol' rusty trombone. But thanks to Slash, I discovered that the guitar was for me, and thus I convinced my parents to allow me to own one. Once I made that mental leap, I threw those other fancy-pants, classical instruments in the metaphorical waste bin. I actually threw my viola bow in the literal trash . . . whoops. And from there, my dutiful yet reluctant father drove me to the guitar shop, where we met a creature from hell.

The shop's proprietor was a very coked-up individual. I didn't have a lot of experience with cocaine at nine or ten, but I've had a lot since, and unless this animal was on methamphetamines, it's safe to say he was well-versed in traversing the snow-covered hills of Mount White Rock. The guy was a tightly wound ball of visceral, unbridled energy, unnatural for a craggy man in his late fifties. I mean, he could've been decades younger. But whatever this guy had been putting into his body, which I'm sure was super good and all, turned him into a barrel-aged beef-jerkied California Raisin of a man.

I had barely entered the shop when I was jump-scared by the Raisin screaming, "*Goddammit!*" then turning to me, not my dad, and continuing on to say, "Sorry, kid. These guitar strings, you gotta be careful with 'em, they'll poke your fuckin' eye out," as he proceeded to tap his glass eye. Likeness to *A Christmas Story*–cum–Bond villain aside, it is true: guitar strings can fuck you up. I took that lesson to heart before taking in the truly grandiose sight that was this store: ceilings fifteen feet high, with electric guitars adorning the walls from floor to ceiling, amplifiers filling and cluttering the entire floor. Up until that moment, I was a Toys R Us kid. But after I laid my eyes on what I assumed were *all* the guitars in the world, this was my new toy store.

I had expected a Gibson Les Paul. I would have also been thrilled with a Fender Stratocaster. Those are still the two big, bad boys on the block. We all want the name-brand shit to flaunt. But then my dad asked crazy Raisin the fateful question, cutting my hopes and dreams to the core: "What is your cheapest guitar?"

Those five words were like a big old butt sitting on my whoopee cushion heart, raspberrying my excitement away with the flappy wisp of a powdered fart. And in response to my dad's inquest, Sir Sniffs-a-Line brought out his most garbage of wares: a Harmony Bobkat H15 with a matching Harmony amplifier—a total of fifty dollars. Now, in today's market, that combination of junk guitar and amp would easily go for a grand. Folks like Jack White really raised the value of the crap gear market. I look back and kick myself for getting rid of the lot. But it was considered junk, at the time. It looked nothing like what Kim Thayil or Mike McCready were playing, but I suppose I was on the path.

Unlike my prior trials with the classically regarded instruments, I took guitar seriously. I played every day. Poorly. But daily. The journey began through acquiring knowledge via a friend's neighbor's dad—a 1 percent biker, home for a weekend to drink in the garage before heading back out on the road, presumably to run guns and murder. He taught me what I consider to be the Holy Grail of punk guitar: the two-finger Ramones chords. This opened a world of possibilities for me, showing how approachable this instrument truly was. If I took two fingers, held them in one simple position, then placed them nearly anywhere on the fretboard, I could basically write a big, dumb three-chord song. I had barely wrapped my head, let alone hands, around the guitar, and I was already off to the races. From there I started learning the entirety of Black Flag's *Nervous Breakdown*, which, at the time, was everything to me.

But my parents wanted me to approach the instrument properly by taking proper lessons. Little did any of us truly understand, at the time, that I was not good at learning the proper way. It's cliché to go on about how neurodivergent types do not flourish in structured environments. But that was the case for me. It rang true in my academics and continued into my musical studies. And it was never more apparent than with my first guitar teacher.

I don't remember his name, but this sandal-wearing jazz a-Phish-ionado reminded me a lot of *Beavis and Butt-Head*'s Mr. Van Driessen—a latter-day hippie, of sorts, with a soft-spoken, spineless demeanor. He had greasy long hair, pulled into a pony-tail, and one extremely long thumbnail on his right hand. That nail gave me the willies. He was like the Freddy Krueger of douchebags. He likely had grown the nail out because he was a traditionally trained jazz bassist, so that nail was for finger pluckin'. But I just wanted to pluck my eyes out every time I was around him. Like the aforementioned cartoon character, he seemed gentle enough, but he became intensely frustrated when I couldn't learn guitar the way he liked to teach it. He was a stickler about the lessons: learn your scales, your positions, your chord formations, and all your theory down to a science. This was not a teacher who relished in the creative; he relished in academics. There was never a question about what music I liked, what I wanted to learn, what players I wanted to emulate. It was no fun. All work. No play. Very dull. Oh boy.

Eventually I was able to convince my parents that, while I loathed this teacher, I still really loved the guitar. I'm certain they were dissatisfied with my seemingly fickle nature, but they could also see that I was struggling with this guy while simultaneously not being ready to give up. And for them, me not giving up was a first.

Teacher number two was found in Evanston, Illinois—the only part of the North Shore that felt with-it and gritty, just a stone's throw away from Chicago. It's been called home by many in the arts, from Steve Albini to Jerry Springer to Grace Slick to Billy Murray to America's sweetheart himself, Kevin Cronin of REO Speedwagon. It houses Northwestern University, full of Smarty-Pants McGee college kids, and thus possesses an additional layer of culture that can only emanate from a renowned school. It also had some of the best, now-defunct, record stores.

Evanston was far cooler than the rest of the sterile, whiter, stuffier nearby towns, like the one I was living in at the time, Winnetka. If you've seen a John Hughes movie, that's Winnetka: wealthy, white, middle of the road. And living in a town like that, as charmed of an existence as it was, left an aspiring loner punk, such as myself, wanting something, anything, more exciting and dangerous.

The Evanston guitar shop, which still stands to this day, aptly named Guitar Works, Ltd., is everything you'd want a guitar shop to be: clean; well put together; run by friendly musicians with no airs; and chock-full of wall-to-wall guitars and basses, a collection of new and used amps, and a repair shop. Plus, they offered lessons, which is how I happened upon who I'd consider my first real guitar teacher, Marshall Dawson.

I recently reached out to Marshall, decades after our initial lessons. I mentioned who I was, my band, and wondered if he even remembered me. I mean, how many students does a guitar teacher go through each year, let alone in twenty-plus years? But not more than a day later, I received an email back from Marshall, which began as follows: "Horn-rimmed glasses, an army coat twice your size, a fondness for Black Flag, and a tendency to lisp slightly when excited? Of course, I remember you!"

I had also shaved my head, in an attempt to look like Ian MacKaye from his Minor Threat years. I was a basic wannabe punk-hardcore bitch. And being remembered this way *truly* warmed my heart. Funny thing is, outside of the glasses and shaved head, I am still more or less the same guy.

I don't know why I hadn't reached out to Marshall sooner. There was a part of me that worried that if he didn't remember me, or just never responded, I would feel hurt. And that's because my time with him was incredibly important. He had a larger impact on my development than either of us realized, not just in my guitar skills but in who I am to this day. Until our recent correspondence, I didn't think he had any idea how much he meant to me.

When we started our lessons, Marshall began by asking me what I was into, musically speaking. He then proceeded to teach me songs. Sure, we worked on rudiments, but it was so much more hands-on and practical. Whether it was an MC5 song, a Hendrix riff, hammer-ons, or just the importance of a solid distortion pedal—a ProCo Rat, to be exact—my lessons were always fun. I think that was the key: fun. I use that word a lot to describe "having a good time," but those are my favorite kinds of time to have. How do you make something that could easily be boring and daunting entertaining? Passion, excitement, high energy—Marshall had all those qualities in spades. And he knew how to make the whole experience quite accessible.

I was, and still am, a self-conscious person, afraid to expose my weaknesses. I didn't love showing anyone how bad I was at guitar, as illogical as that sounds. Because I had barely started, so of course I was bad. Yet Marshall never made me feel lesser than for not knowing what I didn't know. He understood how I liked to learn, by going roundabout, bucking the rules, diving in, and just figuring it out—the way I liked to learn. If it wasn't for Marshall, it's entirely possible I would've given up on the instrument. And then you wouldn't have this book to read! See? We all got something out of those lessons.

To this day, I'm in love with my guitar. Its body. Its neck. The curves. The shape. The sound. The overall safety and comfort the instrument provides me. I have hidden behind a guitar for over two decades, and I will continue to hide behind it until no one cares to see me hide behind one anymore.

I talk a lot yet hate the sound of my voice. That lisp. That nasally, midwestern tone. I can hear my angry mother in it. I can't stand it. I could never be the lead singer of a band. I tried it once, and I was mortified by the results. Find the With Knives *Schadenfreude* EP if you can, and you will see, or hear, what I dare not listen to again. I take no ghoulish joy in hearing myself sing on that record, but maybe you will?

The guitar has always done a better job of talking, and singing, for me than I ever could. It's a truly expressive instrument, one that can convey a vast emotional spectrum. It can cry. It can scream. You can make it laugh. You can be big, dumb, and angry through it. You can be elegant and dainty. Sexy. Ugly. Fat. Skinny. Lazy. Stoned. Stupid. Smart. It can produce endless amounts of sounds to represent the way that you are emoting at that particular time. And the more comfortable you become with the guitar, the more comfortable it becomes with you. And the more comfortable you become with each other, the more you'll notice that the way you perform through the guitar will sound specific to you and you alone. No one will be able to replicate how you express yourself. It will be your sound. Your voice.

I love how accessible the guitar is, the way that almost any aspiring musician can get their hands on one and begin to create. But I suppose, these days, the laptop, and the tools within, are the new guitar for the new generation, for those who have had a difficult time expressing themselves with other instruments. Guitar was that for me. I will always hold it dear as the ultimate form of musical articulation.

It's unfortunate that the instrument has been disregarded in modern times. Some of that was because of the corniest of cornballs, hair guys and nu-metal lunkheads. But mostly, I think the culture just moved on. I am not angry about that—I truly do not wish to be the old man on the hill shouting at a tree to move out of the way so I can get a better view.

Change is inevitable. I used to be part of that change, early on with Fall Out Boy. But now, I'm static, holding on to my guitar for dear life, refusing to allow it to die. I am in one of the last rock bands to have made a hit guitar-based single for pop radio. It makes me sad. Proud too. But overall, I worry the instrument could just become a relic of the past.

But these days I see younger bands, "kids," picking up the instrument, blowing off the dust, and creating new, exciting sounds that will hopefully bring the guitar back into popularity. I suppose everything is cyclical, a wheel that eventually comes around the bend again, bringing back what was once retro and giving it a chance to feel new again, revitalized. I'd like that to happen for the guitar. Whether it's someone shredding, like Vai; digging in fast and chunky, like the Ramones; or anything in between, and beyond, I'd just like to see the next generation give a flying fuck about what I always found to be the coolest thing known to humankind.

The guitar gave me a chance to find myself. And therefore, I'm in love with my guitar.

# Uh, I Think You're in the Wrong Room

I have never felt comfortable, anywhere. Ever. An odd thing to proclaim while writing from perhaps the softest, and seemingly most expensive, couch I've ever laid my buns upon. Jeez, look at the price tag—I think this thing costs more than most cars. It's, like, midrange-luxury priced. What kind would that be? Like, an Acura? Sure. Why not? Who knows? What I do know is this was certainly made by rich jerks, for other, richer jerks—a supple divan, meticulously crafted in the name of soothing the most abraded rumps, correlated with the most affluent of assholes. Bottom line: this fucker is both *super fancy* and *super comfy*.

And yet, as I attempt to settle on what may be the world's most snuggly settee, this rich bag of dog shit (i.e., *moi*) cannot take it easy. It's not just that I feel guilty about the sheer opulence and disgusting excess this love seat represents. Whether it be on a plush throne or a rock-hard recliner, I'm just bad at relaxing. Plus, this isn't my couch. I'm just writing at a furniture store. I didn't think they'd notice, but I can see the saleswoman glowering at me from across the showroom. Maybe I should put my laptop away in the hopes that she will unnotice me?

OK, now I'm bored and staring at some overpriced photo of a beach. Ugh . . . beaches. They make me feel bad too. And exposed. Forced to show off all that skin—all that untanned flesh. My meat is no treat, not for myself or for others. It's private meat. Pale and confidential. And the idea of putting my clean, well-tended feet on hot, grainy, coarse sand makes me queasy. Now I'm all hot and bothered. And so to cool off you expect me to drink this cheap beer I hid in my backpack that will surely give me a pounding headache? An early-onset hangover?

Great, now my anxiety is spinning out because I think that, perhaps, this headache is a tumor—like the one that killed my mom. Thanks, brain! Now I'm just supposed to pretend it's all good and chillax on this imaginary beach. Well, I can't because now I'm going to die. On a fake beach, no less. I'd rather die anywhere else: suffocating in an elevator, bleeding out at the bottom of a canyon, or held hostage in someone's sex dungeon, choking to death on a dirty bandanna. But not on a beach. I hate the beach.

All this beach talk reminds me of those Corona commercials from the late 2000s. Those things stressed me out too. I felt as if they were telling me I had to swallow a singular idea of tranquility—and if I didn't, *I* was the weird one. Now, if you're not familiar with these ads, they were variations of the same thirty-second spot that began with a shot of a gorgeous crystal-clear oceanfront along the coast of the Baja Peninsula with a clear view of the Sea of Cortez. And as the camera slowly pulled back, a perspiring bottle of Corona Extra would reveal itself.

Looking at this drink, you'd immediately know it's cold. *So* damn cold. Its coldness knows no bounds. And this cold beer wants to be inside your sunbaked bod, splashing its refreshing, frothy liquid among your hot, tired organs, which have been pumping extraneous amounts of blood through your flabby, atrophied limbs, working themselves into a tizzy just to help you hit that crucial deadline before landing that well-deserved Cabo vacay.

Man, just take in that beer, the glass bottle beaded with cool, icy perspiration. Not only will this glacial beverage whet your parched palate, but it will also refresh you beyond your wildest dreams. Like an all-inclusive weekend at a wellness retreat, secretly run by an aspiring cult leader, this crisp brew has reached deep into your mind to reveal your inner-outer third eye and rewire your prefrontal cortex. Now you're living in the moment. You can see things that others cannot fathom. Are you Christ himself?

The camera pulls back farther for yet another reveal, and . . . it's you. You're lying on a bamboo lounge chair next to another transcendent soul, separated only by a small side table. And atop this small table are an outdated BlackBerry phone and three smooth stones. Now you're feeling frisky. So you grab a stone. And, with ease, you skip that stone over the pellucid water. Plip. Plop. Ploop. Plump. Four skips? Know what? You rock at rocks. Yeah, I know, it's tight as hell, the way I just used the word "rock" twice. Now, try grabbing another rock and . . . oh, *great*, hear that? Your *dipshit phone* is vibrating. Man, don't we *hate* that thing?

Nothing ruins a nice, quiet holiday like the brutal pangs of modern society. Now, you feel an urge to throw that turd bucket into the Sea of Cortez. In fact, when that needy little piece of electro-trash starts buzzing with its "Please, sir, please answer me now; it's life or death, sir," you start to feel drunk. But not with beer. With rage. You refuse to succumb to the whims of a digitized, Orwellian future where you, a free

human, living in a *perfect* democracy, with thoughts and feelings all your own, never once influenced by any outside con-
glomerate, would ever think to yield your God-given rights to
that of the lowly computer that fits in your palm. No. Time to
do what you do best. Pick up that well-engineered, mostly re-
liable cocksucker and throw it like one of those supersmooth,
badass rocks—right into the ocean. Do it! *Now!* Fuck the fish.
Fuck the whales. Kill your demons.

Holy shit. Are you about to do it? You're picking up the
phone. You're reaching your arm back. Atta boy. You're doing
it. And . . . launch! You did it! Here it goes, we're tracking the
journey; the phone's about to hit the water in three, two . . .
plip. Plop. Ploop. Plump. Plorp? Five skips? Whoa, dude, you
just . . . *threw your phone into the ocean?* Oh my God. All of
your notes are on there. And your big idea for that movie about
you and your frat buddies fucking your way across the lower
forty-eight in an effort to get to DC in time to save the president from a growing army of horny Nazi vampire babes by
using a sun cannon—it's on there! Sure, so is that video of
those same frat "buddies" shoving a bottle inside your body,
asking for ten cents for dutifully "recycling" via the city's "Butthole Depository." *Forget about that.* That's why you drink!
Dammit. Now you're stressed. Come to think of it, were you
ever relaxing? Was this all just a ruse perpetrated by your own
sick mind just to have one final moment of pure, unadulterated
apprehension before you will yourself to walk into the Sea of
Cortez in hopes that a sperm whale will mistake you for a
heaping mass of dense krill and swallow you whole?

Anyway, this is how my mind works. And no, I was not
taken advantage of in college. I barely went to college. God, I
can't relax, even when recalling a twenty-year-old advertisement about relaxing, which most likely none of you remember,

which I turned into a fretful fever dream. Or maybe you do remember? Now I'm stressed that I may have offended your memory. Ah, screw it; it doesn't matter. None of this is about relaxing on a couch or a beach anyway. It's about comfort. And by comfort, I mean within my own skin. I'm talking about day-to-day living. Morning to night, out in the wild, interacting with the world, being "myself."

I've never truly felt settled as me. And that discomfort extends outside my regular, go-about-town life into my larger sphere, defined by my career. But before we get into that, allow me to peel back the Vidalia onion that is my deep-seated psychological neurosis. Take a seat on your regularly priced couch. Get comfy. This will take an unfortunate amount of time.

My dad is a highly accomplished cardiac electrophysiologist. That means not only did he complete kindergarten but he also completed elementary school. Then he went on to high school. And no, no, no—it didn't end there. He *then* went to undergraduate school, and then—get this—he went to graduate school. And that's not all, folks! He then went to the place where doctors become doctor-i-fied: *medical* school. Then he was a resident, doing rounds in emergency rooms, where he saw cool stuff, like a guy blowing his brains out with a revolver. I mean, if it were me, I'd barf, then quit right there and then. But he didn't.

I can't look at my own blood without fainting. One time, when I was getting prepped for a back surgery, I had to get a clot test. This is where a nurse will make a very slight incision on your forearm, then blot the incision with a circular piece of paper to calculate how long it takes your blood to clot. Very simple. So I was in a chair, the nurse had just pinpricked my arm, the slightest puncture, and as she dabbed the paper onto my teensy, tiny cut, I blacked out. The next thing I remember is waking up on the floor, feet up on a pillow, two nurses crouched over me. And just the other week, I had a similar situation, where I tried an at-home food allergy test. To get the results, you pinprick your finger, press four blots of blood onto a sheet, and return said sheet for your results. Again, very simple, and painless. But after one blot, I woke up on the floor of my kitchen, no nurses this time, just my wife and kids, half concerned, half finding it ridiculous . . . because it was. Also, I discovered I'm allergic to summer squash. But suffice it to say, following in my dad's footsteps was impossible. No bloody, no doct-y.

I look up to the big guy, old Richard Gary Trohman. Not just because he watched a person commit a horrific suicide one time and soldiered on, but the man continued to press hard, working his way up, up, up, moving from hospital to hospital, until he landed in Chicago, where he eventually took over running the entire cardiology department. And while doing that, he got bored one day and was like, "Hey, I'll just study to get my MBA, for kicks." No big deal. Just another professional degree. Easy.

That's a lot to live up to. I have a high school diploma. That's it. Yep, you're reading a book written by a person with very little formal education. And that bothers me! Maybe it should bother you. I don't know. Why doesn't it?

I will always have a sort of chip on my shoulder about this, regardless of the fact that, on paper, I've outperformed my dad in that I have made more money. Sure. Money. That means nothing. I'll always feel lesser than my father because I never went to a school for higher learning and received a piece of paper from that institution that says, "You took out half a million dollars in loans, and now you're smart because we said so!"

Yes, while I have my head fully wrapped around that irony, the irony itself is wrapped around that first irony, creating a feedback loop of ironic uncomfortable self-loathing. I am not sure I will ever truly feel capable of seeing myself as a big, smart boy without that stupid piece of paper. And that's no one's fault; it's probably some combination of my own depressive disorder mixed with outmoded societal expectations that one is not intelligent without a document from a prestigious university saying so.

My dad never made me feel like a ding-a-ling for not finishing school. In fact, he's very proud of me. I couldn't have asked for a more supportive parent. He allowed me to drop out of college, with barely a quarter of a semester under my belt, to pursue Fall Out Boy. He understood that I only had one chance to see if this whole "band thing" would work. And it worked. I mean, I can only assume you're reading this because it worked. And if you're reading this because the book was well reviewed, well hot dog! Glad I bought this book-writing robot monkey!

Speaking of money well spent, I clearly saved my parents hundreds of thousands of dollars by *not* going to school. You're welcome! They only had to spend *maybe* a grand, total, on what led to my career in music. Passion, while in short supply, is free. And passion is what set me on the path to become a guitarist, full-time.

As I've gushed, I love the instrument to death, although I'm not half the player I wish I were, nor can I play like any of my heroes. And yet somehow, against all odds, I play professionally. At about the highest level too. Yet even after decades of riffing in bands, I still feel like a fake, a fraud, a charlatan—a feeling further bolstered by playing in other bands with guys like Scott Ian, one of the fastest right hands in guitar, period—a true thrash metal legend. I can't hold a candle to that guy. Or consider my friendship with Brendon Small, the creator and one-man band behind the animated series *Metalocalypse*—a Berklee-trained guitarist who can play stratospheres around me. While neither of these wonderful friends have *ever* made me feel like I shouldn't be where I am, they're just better. It's objectively true. And so this leaves me to wonder why *I'm* the guy playing guitar in the much bigger band and not *them*. I realize there's more than just technical ability involved, but it still doesn't seem fair or deserved. And yet.

I have an affliction, a common one shared by many in the creative community. One could say that this affliction is connected to my clinical mental illness, but I don't think it's unique to me. This impostor syndrome, it's something I will never shake—the idea that I should not be where I am. I have this burning notion that I am not qualified to be doing what it is that I am doing for a living.

I find it remarkably bizarre that I get paid to play guitar, and handsomely, as a vocation. And right now, as I am crafting this chapter that you, dear reader, are dearly reading, I am amid the traveling circus known as a *tour*, performing my craft at a stadium level, with two bands that have informed my own playing and career—Green Day and Weezer. Compounded by the guilt that I should not be playing guitar professionally is the shame I feel being sandwiched between two massive artists that have enlightened my musical upbringing. It feels undeserved. I was a child when these acts came onto the scene, helping to thrust me toward my eventual guitar-dom. And now my band, the one I helped establish out of teenage desperation, is somehow considered of the same ilk. I am simultaneously both honored and full of concern that, again, I should not be here.

It's not that I don't feel I've worked hard to get where I'm at. I may not have inherited my father's degrees, but I did inherit his intense, unhealthy work ethic. And I will do what it takes, within the realm of morality, to succeed, or at the very least get to the point where everyone says, "Please, no more. Time to stop now." Even then, I may not quit. But even if I do succeed in all the trials, make it to the final round, pass the exam, and become inducted into the Professional Men, Women, and So Forth Club, at the end of the day I would still feel that I do not deserve to be here.

I know some would disagree about the way I pitifully doubt the validity of my stature. For those about to disagree, I salute you. And those with hate in your heart who would fully agree with me that I should be cast into a pit of fire so that a new, more worthy challenger could replace me, sure. Why not?

I have always felt like the guy that bullshitted his way into the room. Like the protagonist in Cameron Crowe's *Almost Famous*, I relate more to the William Millers of the world, the wide-eyed, bushy-tailed kids who can't believe they're hanging out with the rock stars, and suckers of rock stars. They know they shouldn't be where they are, and yet they're where they are. So why fuck it up and throw in the towel? Just roll with it, man.

As I got older, I started to look outside of music, in hopes of pursuing alternate creative ventures in order to discover more about myself and attempt to murder my impostor syndrome along the way. But like cancer cells in the bloodstream, my malady would continue to rear its ugly head in more insidious ways.

When I made the commitment to dive into something totally new, totally outside the band-sphere, I did it alone. Up until then, I had only known working with bandmates, a group, a team. If one fails, we all fail. So it's scary to plunge solo, headfirst into a new profession, one with an equal lack of certainty and similarly low success rate as music. To do so is putting yourself through hell once more, unnecessarily. I have money, so why do it all over again? An insatiable ego? This "need" to create? Mental twistedness? A death wish? All of the above and so much more?

Carving out a secondary career path, going at it on my own, forced me to confront my ongoing battle with my internal enemies, the *real* haters, in an effort to find a sense of identity and some overdue confidence.

In the midst of Fall Out Boy's much-needed hiatus, between the years 2010 and 2012, I was living in New York: the Big Apple. The City That Never Sleeps. Empire City. Gotham City. The City So Great, They Named It After the State? The State So Pretty, They Named It After the City? The Place Where I Once Saw a Man Masturbate Sensually in Broad Daylight on Houston Street Adjacent to Tweens Playing Basketball. NYC.

Attempting to find my own footing outside of being "that other guy from Fall Out Boy," I tried my hand at the world of commercial scoring. I worked with companies that would farm out various original pieces, on spec, in hopes of landing some national ad campaigns. I know, *very* punk. But I never claimed to be very punk. Don't let the tattoos fool you.

You see, I had grown tired of touring, which is how people in bands make money. Fall Out Boy was on the road over two hundred days a year. Even my short tenure with the hard-rock supergroup The Damned Things felt exacting and arduous for someone who, at a young age, had already been touring for well over a decade. I was exhausted. I just wanted to be with my wife, in my tiny Manhattan apartment, wake up in the same place every day, and have some sort of routine. I thought it'd be good for my ailing back and my persistent mental problems to feel human. I thought maybe I'd want to kill myself a *little* less if I wasn't in so much physical and existential pain. I shrugged, cautiously optimistic at the thought that it was possible.

So I concocted a plan, which was that I would make the transition from writing music with my bands to scoring compositions for TV and film. Seemed like a logical, albeit difficult, leap. I knew I'd have to find a way into that world. See, even a guy from a large band can't just walk into a room and yell, in a big dumb idiot voice, "Durr, I'd like to score a movie now!" Because the person in the room, the one in charge, would just reply, "Um, ma'am, this is a Wendy's." And I'd remove the long hair from my face; then the cashier would shriek, discovering how ugly of a ma'am I am. I'd then stomp out of that Wendy's, leaving wholly frustrated, gripping a deliciously greasy bag of chicken. The cashier would continue on: "Ma'am, that's not yours. Ma'am! *Ma'am!*"

I can't just get a fancy new job because I currently hold a fancy old job. No matter what level you make it to in one field, you must prove yourself in a new one if you'd like to exist there, let alone subsist, whatsoever. At least, that's how it works for guys like me, Z-level celebrities, the guy behind the guy, behind the guy, behind the guy, and so on, that everyone says, "Wait, are you with those guys?"

So I began my short-lived tenure as a commercial music man, hoping I'd eventually rack up so many spots that I'd have a burning-hot calling card that I could use to sear my way into Tinseltown scoring. Looking back on it all, I'm pretty sure this was not the correct path to follow. No one hires the Meow Mix guy to score a Paul Thomas Anderson film, or a Wes

Anderson film, or even a bumper for *Anderson Cooper 360*. But I didn't know where to start. I didn't know who to ask. Despite my years in the music industry, I had very few connections in Hollywood. But I did have some friends who had ways in at these strange places, referred to as jingle houses, companies that collect original music in hopes of placing said music in various commercials. This seemed like my in! I was prolific when it came to creating music, and I was happy to do the hard work and prove to everyone that I had what it takes. I was going to land every ad for Cialis out there, even if it cost me my own erectile functioning.

So I played the game. I submitted for all sorts of jobs, hunkering down in the smallest of the two bedrooms within my teensy West Village abode. I had converted this glorified closet into a makeshift recording studio, consisting of a beat-up laptop, budget speakers, a couple of guitars, and a bass. People have done more with less.

I can't remember most of what I vied for, but I failed to get the majority of the jobs. However, I did get very close to landing a Super Bowl commercial. The folks at either the jingle house or the NFL had requested a Philip Glass time-lapse style piece to overlay atop slo-mo football players playing with footballs and such; I'm not a sportsman, but I've been around the block, and I know what types of balls these guys fancy. Bottom line: whoever requested this music wanted Philip Glass quality without paying Philip Glass money. And I thought, who better to be the sixth-tier budget Philip Glass than me, Joe Trohman, a much lesser-regarded Jewish musician.

I created a Glass-like measure for my prospective bosses or whatever mysterious Wizard of Oz type I was trying to appease. And you know what? The faceless entities at fill-in-the-blank place loved it! In fact, they wanted me to take my spec and add twice as much score, meaning they just wanted me to double it. Yeah, baby! Twice as nice! Now I just had to deliver, and I'd have my big break into the rewarding medium that unites the aural and visual arts, thus satisfying the creative soul to its core: corporate advertisement!

So I delivered. And I waited. And waited. And waited some more. At that time in my life, I had a lot of time to wait; I was newly married, with no children and a surplus of marijuana nuggies, so I spent my days waking, baking, and playing video games until I went into my shoebox studio and recorded music into the void. I was primed to waste time. Then, after my seventh or eighth wait, I finally heard from the jingle house. It was time! Time to officially say that I've landed . . . nothing. Yes, it turns out that all that work, all that waiting, was to discover that the music for this Super Bowl ad would in fact be a previously existing piece written and recorded by none other than Philip Glass, a much better-regarded Jewish musician.

Some would give up upon hearing that news. I laughed, as I was *very* high. But over the course of the next couple of years, as I stopped being as high and started going back to making records and touring with Fall Out Boy, I started to think about my future career as a wannabe composer. And then, when I got my wife pregnant with our first girl, the glorious Ruby Sioux, I thought more about that wannabe career.

I considered the fact that I was in New York and that Hollywood, where the films and TV were being put together, was in California, which was not in New York but on the other side of the country. I considered that being closer to that industry may allow me to actually, potentially, embed myself within said industry—the Hollywood Tinseltown Successful Film and TV Hotshots Industry, Inc., LLC. And truthfully, with a baby on the way, I had more reason to want to find an alternate career in which I could still make music and not travel so much, so I could be home with my new kiddo. So I suggested to my wife, Marie, that we move to California, the place that is on fire a lot. It wasn't on fire as much then. So she said yes.

After one year of living in Los Angeles, I learned two things: (1) I don't hate LA. In fact, I really love it. I used to think it was an awful place, but it's not—you just need to find your thing amid the vast urban sprawl. My wife and I, as two early-thirtysomethings, found that "thing" on the East Side, an area preordained for "hip" New York transplants. Or in our case, ex-Chicagoans masquerading as "hip" New York transplants.

Oh, and (2) the other thing. Well, that turned out to be that I hate composing for film and TV. I tried my hand at it for that first year after we moved to LA. I fully realize that a year of trying something as difficult as composing for the screen is not enough time to see if that something will come to fruition, but I quickly learned that it was not for me. I did some spots for cable networks, a little commercial work, some theme songs for awards shows, but it was thankless and, truthfully, the worst possible way for me to create music.

Up to that point, I had spent the past fifteen years of my life making and performing my own songs, the way my bandmates and I intended. We had called a lot of the shots. I became accustomed to making music that way. So naturally I didn't like making it for other people, based on their stipulations, which were understandably to service something greater than my "art." But it clearly became too difficult for me to make music any other way than my way. And so there went my composing ambitions.

Funny thing is, the moment I decided that I was done with the whole scoring pipe dream hullaballoo, I was offered a meager, albeit fun and challenging, composing gig. I refer to it as a "gig" because it wasn't a job. A job pays enough to afford things, and this paid little, if anything, which was all fine and well. This gig was not about the money. My close friend and The Damned Things bandmate Keith Buckley had just written a book of his own, an engaging tome with both fictional and semiautobiographical elements, *Scale*, and he had come to me in hopes I could record the audiobook. To boot, the book's publisher had just gotten into the habit of releasing audiobooks on vinyl, accompanied by a score. And since Keith and I have a fun, relaxed musical relationship, he asked if I would be interested in scoring the thing. Without a thought, I said yes. Because he's Keith. He's my friend. We have fun together. You know how I feel about fun.

But I like to make things difficult for myself, so I conceived this saga-like composition in which I would give each chapter its own individual music piece. So that meant coming up with over twenty different instrumental segments for the audiobook on vinyl. Sounds like a fun idea and all, but consider the fact that twenty-plus chapters of an audiobook amounts to at least three films' worth of score, maybe more. As soon as I carved out this undertaking, I realized I'd made a mistake, and I could not do the audiobook alone without missing the deadline and possibly thrusting myself into some sort of stress-induced coma. So I enlisted the help of another pal, Josh Newton, who also played in The Damned Things and was, for a time, my guitar tech in Fall Out Boy. Together, we did it. And it came out well. I am proud of it. And *no one* heard it, as labors of love tend to go unnoticed.

So with the project complete, and very much ignored, I was once again at a point in my life where I felt uncertain about who I was and where I was going. For a bit, I faltered, emotionally speaking. Yes, I was the guitarist in a large band. But I am a person who likes to make things, and I love having things to make. And within Fall Out Boy, I am not the chief "maker." Yadda, yadda, you heard it before.

So here I was, in my early thirties, a new dad, living in a new city, trying to redefine who I was. It felt weird and lonely, but not hopeless. Just confusing. I had this unearned confidence that the universe would somehow reveal itself to me and thus work out. Perhaps it was all the therapy and medication keeping me in check, but I had a feeling something would happen. And that's when I met, or really remet, the person who would change my trajectory entirely and, in a strange way, pull me out from my tightly wrapped burrito comprising seven layers of beans, cheese, and shredded self-hatred.

It takes a certain kind of person to lift you from the depths of your own personal hell. I am not a religious man, I am not a man of Christ, and I've never served in the clergy, as far as I'm aware, but Brandon Dermer might as well be my guardian angel. You see, soon after my fifth bout of spiritual emptiness, post–scoring Keith's audiobook, Keith and I commemorated our collective feat with a very fun, very poorly attended performance at a record store in central Hollywood. At this performance, to *seven* people, Keith read an excerpt from his novel as I accompanied the reading with some ethereal, ill-conceived, stoner guitar riffs—music soaked in reverb and delay to make it all *seem* complex. Side note for aspiring, apathetic guitarists: effects are a great way to hide all mistakes and afford a sense of snobbery wherein it seems like you own, and celebrate, all the latter, painful Radiohead albums.

It was at this little show in LA where I became reacquainted with Brandon Dermer, not just one of seven audience members but also a fellow Chicagoan and onetime pop-punker who manifested his own destiny to the West Coast as an up-and-coming director/writer. He had worked at various Paramount-owned networks while doing tons of visually stunning and conceptually brilliant music videos with all sorts of artists, from Diplo to Panic! at the Disco, and eventually my own group, The Damned Things, with good old Keith.

Brandon had connected with Keith because, at one point, on the internet, there was a small-time meme pointing out the fact that Keith looked a lot like comedian/musician Jon Lajoie, known for portraying Taco on FX's TV show *The League*, created by writer/director Jeff Schaffer, renowned for concocting *Seinfeld*'s Festivus pole. How many Kevin Bacons is that? Anyway, Brandon had been working on Lajoie's music videos, and being a big Every Time I Die fan himself, he reached out to Keith to see if he'd like to do a sketch of sorts with Lajoie, to highlight their doppelgänger-ness.

This is how Keith and Brandon became friends. And that's what led Brandon to the lightly attended reading at the now-defunct record store. And so Keith introduced me to Brandon, and it turned out that Brandon's old teenage band had opened for a very fresh-faced Fall Out Boy at the local youth organization in Winnetka, Illinois. While I honestly don't remember that show, or meeting Brandon before, I was extremely excited to talk about the old days and connect with someone from that time and place in my life, back when doing the band was literally only a blast—zero pressure, zero money.

And so as the night progressed, I discovered that Brandon and I had more in common than just a minor shared history—we really hit it off. I normally love to talk about things Chicago related, but it was when we started getting deep into film and television that the real connection became apparent. I'd always been passionate about film and TV but had never attempted to become a filmmaker, producer, comedian, screenwriter, or anything within that field. It never crossed my mind that I could or should. It's a vast medium that I truly love and care about, and perhaps that was, to a degree, why I never wanted to muck it up. I didn't want to get my dirty fingerprints all over it. It also felt big, terrifying, and too much for little ol' me to approach.

As I've mentioned, some of my first memories of film were watching movies like *The Omen* with my mother when I was in elementary school. And my dad made sure to instill in me the tenets of both Monty Python and Mel Brooks. I also remember that once, during middle school spring break, I took some of my dad's other film recommendations to heart and spent the whole break watching *The Last Temptation of Christ*, *Full Metal Jacket*, Andy Kaufman compilations, *The Warriors*, and *Rumble Fish*. My mom took me to see *Sling Blade* when I was twelve and *The Blair Witch Project* when I was fifteen. That same year, I snuck into three different theaters to see *Eyes Wide Shut*, not because I was a horny teen but because I was a huge Kubrick fan. I was also a horny teen. Not mutually exclusive.

As I was growing up, we were the family with the TV on *all* the time. I was of the last generation to watch true laugh-track-laden, multi-cam sitcoms like *Family Matters* and *Step by Step*. I watched *The X-Files* religiously. I also thoroughly enjoyed hearkening back to the times of old, losing myself in hours upon hours of *The Twilight Zone* and *Alfred Hitchcock Presents*.

And back in the day, Nickelodeon had Nick at Nite, where I was exposed to *Mork & Mindy*; *Taxi*; *I Dream of Jeannie*; *Welcome Back, Kotter*; *The Odd Couple*; *Get Smart*; *Laverne & Shirley*; and *M\*A\*S\*H*, among others. My dad and I *loved* watching *M\*A\*S\*H*, so much so that I eventually bought him the entire series on VHS—seventy-one tapes in all. I suppose I did not anticipate the existence of Hulu, but I don't regret it. That set is tactile!

*The Simpsons* were probably the first TV family I found on my own, and I still celebrate them to this day, even with my own kids. Despite the past two decades of *Simpsons* sadness, the first eleven or so seasons are incredible! There was also the '90s Nick stuff, like *The Ren & Stimpy Show* and *Rocko's Modern Life*. And then there was *Seinfeld*, the quintessential show about "nothing," but really it was just a show about living in New York, foibles, and Jewish idiosyncrasies. That felt like a show for me—comedy derived from old-world Jewish humor, tailor-made for a darkly strange Jewish kid from a darkly strange old-world Jewish family from New York.

This is what Brandon and I talked about for at least two hours, possibly more—our deep and genuine love for all things written for the screen, small and large. And I knew we were really getting somewhere, becoming fast friends, once we hit it hard over two life tenets: John Carpenter and *Mr. Show*, the former a benchmark for knowing whether someone really loves horror and the latter for whether someone really gets comedy.

So as the night progressed, I, a onetime problem drinker, got drunker and began to do what I do when I get problem drunk, which is say problematic things. And within these problematic things, I had apparently, brashly, proclaimed my staunch opinions on film, TV, and especially comedy, as if I deserved to have any opinion on any of it, whatsoever.

Considering I had no clear recollection of the events, I called up Brandon to ask what he thought of my proclamations so I could get him on the record and embarrass myself properly. According to him, I sounded like someone who knew what I was talking about and understood how things in "the biz" worked. That's very nice of him to say, since I was full of crap. How could I not have been? I had never worked in "the biz." But considering "the biz" is famous for being full of crap, perhaps I was inching toward the right place, toward the right thing. And Brandon felt I was somebody worth his time.

As we continued to forge our friendship, Brandon, ever the enthusiastic pusher, more than suggested that I come with him to meet his TV lit manager. I did not want to do this. I had friends in the comedy world, writers, stand-ups, et al., who had proposed ideas that we write something together or work on a project in some capacity. I had always said no. I felt, as a career musician, and an average one at best, that it would be sacrilege to jump into their lane and try to do what they do. I love comedy. I love horror. I love television. I love film. And I respect what my friends in the industry do too much. I did not want to cover their stuff in my viral bile, thus ruining it for all.

But Brandon would not accept the idea that I wouldn't at the very least just take a drive to his manager's office and have a conversation.

"What about?" I snottily asked.

"Just a chat; it'll be fun," he promised.

It didn't sound fun. I hate offices. Not so much because they are boxes, much like prison cells. But as I would with a prison, I enter an office wondering, "What group of people should I align myself with, for safety?" I then realize there is no group for me. That's when I brace myself for the office gang rape. But outside of those rational fears, Brandon and I were already having fun, having a conversation, right then and there, free of the woes of incarceration. Yet he badgered me further and further, insisting that I "had the goods, kid," and that it would be worth talking about working within that world, the difficult, failure-ridden, sick, and twisted world of writing for television, in which I had no prior experience or skill set.

In hindsight, Brandon, a true sweetheart, was pushing me because he saw something in me that I refused to see at the time. But I felt like such an impostor in music that I didn't need to compound that feeling in yet another medium, one that I had not yet ruined whatsoever for myself or anyone else. I really did not want to jump into that world in any capacity. But Brandon has a way of convincing you that the impossible is possible, and in such a genuine, nonmanipulative way. He knew that I was the type of person who would regret it if I didn't, at the very least, inspect the situation, kick the tires, and see what the heck was going on. And I don't like missed opportunities. I have terrible FOMO.

So cut to a day later, and I'm sitting with his manager, discussing all things television, not really concerned one way or another, just being honest and making sure it was *very* clear that I was very aware that I did not know what I was talking about. Apparently, during this conversation, I had pitched an idea. Whoops. For some reason, this idea had impressed Brandon's manager. And then that idea made its way through the company, ending up with another writer/director they represent—somebody very prominent in the world of comedy, film, and TV. I won't divulge this guy's name, but I'll say that he's both a legend and a hero of mine, someone who graciously opened himself up to me with no judgment whatsoever. If you can figure out who this person is from that description . . . well, then you're a real cock of the roost, and we're *all* impressed. Fuck you.

Anyhoo! Brandon and I developed a TV show with this comedy legend for a couple of years, which ultimately fell apart. But within that time, I had read every script I could get my hands on, studied every book I could buy, and listened intently to every single person in the industry who was willing to divulge delicious, savory, breaded nuggets of wisdom. I took it fucking seriously. Apparently, I liked the challenge. And I like writing. I suppose, from watching all that TV, I understood, well enough, how to construct story, characters, farts, heart, the whole shebang. Enough to get started on a long road to failure, at least.

And whatever I didn't know, which was a lot, I was fortunate enough to have folks show me, to walk me through the right and wrong way to approach each painstaking, sometimes totally moronic, situation that you come across when developing television. And let me tell you—developing TV is a thankless endeavor in which you get paid nothing to maybe sell one thing, *if* you sell anything at all. And *if* you sell something, that thing will likely *never* get made. It's not a formula for success, even if you're in some stupid big band.

But being in my stupid big band has undoubtedly helped me get through doors that would normally be closed to others in my nascent position. Regardless, once I walk in the door, I can't just yell, "Hi, I'm in Fall Out Boy; give me a TV show, duuuurp a doo!" I mean, I guess I could. But that's what everyone would expect a guy like me to do. I would expect a guy like me to do that. However, while maybe I don't have my father's degree, I have a modicum of his intellect and caution, just enough to trick people into thinking I'm one-quarter not stupid.

A pompous executive (is that tautology?) at a studio once asked me, "Why? Why try to work your way into a business this difficult when you've already made it in another difficult business?" I'm paraphrasing it much friendlier than he put it. But what he didn't understand is my aforementioned need to create. And I have somehow found a group of people in this business—dear friends who I look up to, like Brian Posehn (literally) and Seth Green, who like what I do enough to want to nurture my creations, people who are in this business for the same reasons as myself, to make cool shit.

And I do want to make TV—said everyone with delusions of grandeur. I love TV. I care about TV. Sure, the boob tube rots the brain, but who needs those things? Too pink and squishy, I say. And I've worked my tush off to try to get people to want to make TV with me. I've even gotten close a few times. I've sold some shows, animated ideas primarily, such as one called *Superdown*, about a guy who only gets superpowers when he's super depressed. Shocker. I also developed countless duds, like *Born-Again Tristan*, a series about a teenager named Tristan who grew up in a religious family, of Satanists, who does not want to be evil anymore but wants to do good. Get it? It's a play on words! Yuk-a-duk-a-dee! Even now I am in the midst of producing a pilot, and I have to assume that it'll never see the light of day. But I'm having fun doing it. Like a prehistoric bird being used as a carjack for a slate rock convertible, it's a living!

Knowing the failure rate, I keep trying. And I don't feel like I belong here either. My presence is a disservice to those who have been here more than twice as long as I have, grinding, working just as hard, if not harder, and with far fewer advantages than myself. It's probably also a disservice to those who are successful too. Without a doubt, I do not deserve to be here. But I guess I don't feel like I belong anywhere. And I also don't really care what you think. (Even though I also care what you think. Ahh, my brain! Get it out of here.) It doesn't really matter, though. Like playing in a band, working in TV is a form of intense creative collaboration that boils down to yet another reason to hang out with my friends, make one another laugh, and try to get important people with money to pay us to make our dumb idea that we think is better than everyone else's dumb idea.

# Pregnant Musings from an
# Infertile Man

I was going to vomit, then pass out. Or pass out, then vomit. Either way, if I didn't make it to my bed in time, there was a good chance I was going to hit my head on my dresser before collapsing onto the floor. With that in mind, I projected the following: first the yucky vomit, then the fainting, then the fall—*slam!*—with the hitting of the head on the railing, then the passing out, followed by the bleeding out, then the slow, agonizing death, then the arrival at the afterlife, where I'd have to answer for my sins to some sort of "higher power" managing the crossroads demarcating heaven from hell.

But I wouldn't have my answers, would I? I don't believe in a higher power. Big mistake, buddy. It seems like all that nonbelieving has really thrust me into what some may call "a snag." I never prepared for this moment, the moment of truth.

So this higher power—let's call him Steve—he's all high-and-mighty-like, chastising me: "What do you have to say for all these sins? *Especially* the masturbation."

And I'd shrug, feeling all exposed and put on the spot. Then I'd defensively, superciliously reply, "I dunno, *Steve*. I guess I like to jerk off. Is that a crime?"

And he'd say, "Yes."

So I'd spend my eternity in hell, relegated to some sort of humiliating, repetitive job, like power washing demon anuses, making life insurance cold calls, or maybe something to do with Peter Thiel. Probably that, the Thiel thing. That seems worse than buttholes. Or maybe it'll still involve buttholes. I don't mean because he's gay; I just mean he might have me clean his butthole.

Before the fainting, I had yelled downstairs to my wife that I was about to faint. I don't think she heard me. It's entirely possible that I only imagined yelling. My vision was pinning. Thankfully, I made it to the bed in the nick of time.

I'm vasovagal, which means if I catch the sight of blood (usually my own) or am exposed to some physically or emotionally distressing situation, I'll get intense nausea, go pale, then almost instantly lose consciousness. And the fainting episode was courtesy of Zayda Mae, my spicy, at the time, three-year-old.

Zayda's a fighter. And I mean that as a compliment—the child does not take shit from no one. And that fighter's spirit was kicked directly into my already very swollen testicles. Lord, I had never felt pain like that. Sure, I'd been kicked, hit, punched, whacked, snapped, slapped, whipped, and even aggressively tapped upon my nards. But this was on another level. And no, I know what you're thinking: I did *not* get scrotal enhancement surgery. No, no. See, just a week prior, I had opted for just the opposite, a type of elective scrotal de-enhancement surgery. Those of us in the know call it a "nut job." But for the plebs, I had just recently received my first, and theoretically last, vasectomy.

It wasn't Zayda's fault that I was in this predicament—the hideous pain or the vasectomy. She and I were playing, and I miscalculated how long her legs had gotten as of late; little kids love to grow. So one thing led to another, and there I was, bowled over, wondering whether her tiny, powerful feet had torn apart the innards of my sack.

I hadn't been dying to get the vasectomy. Not that I had intended to bequeath a quiverfull of children. But as I've explained, I don't do well with blood and physical sensitivity. So one could imagine that the idea of scientifically slicing the old cobblers to bits, attacking the most sensitive part of a man's body, gave me both night- and daymares. However, the whole kit ended up not being too bad, thanks to a big, fat Valium before the procedure, and lemme tell you, once that bad Larry kicked in, I would've let that doctor cut off all the balls, the whole penis, the arms, the legs, whatever. I did not care. Plus, considering my wife had gone through the trouble of destroying her own genitals, via pushing out the two most amazing kids in the world (in my humble opinion), the least I could do was have my testicles professionally mutilated so we wouldn't end up with an unplanned third child.

I had always wanted to become a parent. Not in the same way my wife had, espousing her fantasies about the curly-haired half-Jewish boy we might have one day—a mini-Joe. I enjoyed hearing her sweet suppositions but did not fantasize about those things myself. I didn't imagine my future children; I don't know if basic-bitch straight guys do that. Maybe some do? My dreams were very attainable and shortsighted: hoping the weed guy would pick up his phone to help make the Chinese food I had just ordered twice as delicious.

But I had grown up in a household with a father who genuinely loved being a dad. And though I also had a mother who often told me things like "I hate my life," while burning two large, eyeball-shaped holes through my cranium, I was lucky to have choices. So I chose to look up to my dad. He was my model for the possibility that one day I might become a decent father myself.

For a great deal of my life, I wanted to *be* my dad. Sure, Slash was my "delusions of grandeur" hero, but Dr. Richard Gary Trohman, MD, was my grounded, physical, attainable hero. He was somebody I could see myself being, one day. Like him, I wanted to eventually have my own serious career. And like him, I considered the notion that one day I too would want kids of my own.

I started touring in bands as a child, myself. Fifteen years old, as you have undoubtedly been made to understand fifteen-plus times by this point. Then, about four years later, two to three years after Fall Out Boy started, music had become a sort of job that could pay the rent, pay my utilities, afford me my life-affirming CDs at Tower Records, and help to chip away at my mounting Thai food bills. But despite living on my own in the city of Chicago and paying my own way, I was still a kid. And it was around this time that I met my future wife, Marie—also a kid, a kid in undergraduate school trying to figure out what her not-kid life would amount to.

Marie was roommates with an old high school pal, which is how I ended up a strange boy in her dorm room. She wasn't expecting me. Nor did it seem she wanted me there. Marie was in a rush to get from one class to another, and I was in no rush, in between tours, sitting on my friend's bed, having just returned from an ill-fated attempted trip to New York. Fall Out Boy was supposed to film a music video there, for a song off *Take This to Your Grave*. But instead of making a music video, this is when we hit that black ice en route, somewhere in Pennsylvania, and crashed into a forest.

Time does slow down when you think you're about to die. I remember having driven throughout the night, in sleet, rain, and snow. It was treacherous. I thought I was going to be the one to kill us. But I did my allotted five or so hours behind the wheel, then handed the reins off to our tour manager at the time. It was a clear, crisp winter morning when he took over, and we went skidding off the highway, into the trees. It was a fifteen-passenger Dodge Ram van. I was sleeping on the front bench. I don't remember flying off the seat or anything, but I do remember all the windows instantaneously shattering upon impact. Our attached trailer, carrying all of our gear, was destroyed, as were the twenty or so boxes of merchandise, mainly T-shirts. And, of course, the van was totaled. Yet no one had a scratch on them, or even seemed bothered, outside of Andy, who had momentary shock postwreck.

After spending hours and hours sorting out the details of the crash, the rest of the band, and our small crew, traveled back home to the Midwest. But I ventured forth to NYC, to visit a girl in Jersey who I thought I had been dating, but I don't think she had the same idea. A few years older than myself, she wasn't fully sold on me—the frenzied, inexperienced youngster. And near the end of my visit, things imploded; I don't know exactly if we "broke up" or if the amorphous, semi-romantic rapport fell apart due to my own neurosis and poor behavior. Or perhaps I was just too childish. Regardless, it was a nonstarter, and quite toxic for the both of us. I thought I was going to feel horrible when it ended, but I felt great. Whatever we weren't, we were for certain not "it" anymore. And I was free to spend the next couple of days on my own.

After being kicked out of her house, I putzed about the city for the next two days. I paid for a hotel room in cash, as I had yet to procure a credit card, and at one point I saw Quentin

Tarantino being driven around, to which I exclaimed, "That's Quentin Tarantino!" That reminded me a lot of a "story" my dad liked to tell. The lore goes that he once saw the rapper Coolio walking somewhere. So he approached Coolio and asked, "Are you Coolio?" And Coolio replied, "Yes." That's the story! Coming full circle, realizing I was indeed metamorphosizing into my father, I decided the fun was over and it was time to book a flight home.

Back in the Second City, I found myself sitting on my friend's dorm room mattress when the most beautiful girl I had *ever* seen walked into the room. She was in a huff. And I was too vapid at the time to see outside of myself, to realize this woman was busy, too busy to pay me, a total unknown, any mind. But I did not care. Not in the least. People often romanticize the love-at-first-sight trope. Usually, that feeling of "love" just amounts to intense lust, leaving behind a wave of hate and pubic shellfish or under-the-pants sores in its wake. But as someone ten years into a marriage, one that I feel is probably as happy as a happily married man, such as myself, could ever get, I can say that seeing Marie for the first time was, without a doubt, the full realization of that trope. I was in love. And I was ready to make my move.

Until that moment in my life, I was afraid to take risks, especially in the dating sphere. Outside of the young woman that I had just messily, sort of, maybe broken up with, the only other dating experience I'd had, up to that point, was in high school, with a sweet girl who also happened to be the school's mascot. And she asked *me* out. But then she dumped me. It was devastating; not even the school mascot wanted me. However, I also knew the dissolution was 100 percent my fault, as she had clearly wanted me to assert some sort of dominance, make some moves, get touchy, get kissy, et cetera and so forth.

But I, being a timid, spindly nerd with zero sexual experience or confidence, was not going to be able to give her "the goods," as some may put it. Others may not. I certainly wouldn't.

The clear lesson I could have taken away from that moment was that I'd be far better off risking it once in a while, rather than nervously doing nothing. But it took a few more years to sort out that courage, until Marie entered my orbit, waking up my long-dormant nerve. As she strode into the room, my inner voice began nagging at me: "Say something, you fucking moron, or you will regret this for the rest of your insignificant, worthless life, which will amount to *nothing* if you do not engage in conversation. Now."

He's not nice, my inner voice, but he gets stuff done! And so as Marie hastily threw her backpack on her mattress and took out some textbooks to replace them with others, I approached and brilliantly stated, "Hey. Nice shoes." It's true—I really did like her shoes, and also, I had no game. They were Le Coq Sportif, French running shoes emblazoned with a rooster. While recollecting this story, I misremembered the shoes as branded with the word "Cock." Rooster. Cock. Cock. Rooster. Of course, my brain went penile. But I figured it out, eventually. Anyway, Marie's response to my inane, reaching compliment was a flippant "Uh, thanks?" complete with no eye contact as she hustled out of the room. And that was it. I was smitten. She wanted nothing to do with me, and I wanted everything to do with her.

I spent the next few years gradually courting Marie, showing her I was genuinely interested in her mind and personality just as much as her face and body and rooster shoes. And once Marie began to trust that I was not just some repulsive band guy trying to get into her pants for a one-night stand to regale my buddies with, we began dating seriously. Then, after about three years of that phooey, we became engaged, moved to New York, and eventually entered the whole matrimony business. From ages twenty to twenty-seven, we covered a lot of ground. And looking back on it, I couldn't imagine it any other way.

Cut to eight or so years after meeting, just a year into marriage, and we hit that sort of wall, a "What do we do next?" query that I assume many married couples run into. It's a crossroads of sorts, one where, as a team, you choose whether to stay selfish or spawn. There's nothing wrong with staying selfish. You can continue to drink, drug, party, and spend money on yourselves for eternity. Plus, you don't add to the planet's population crisis. No judgment there. But you can also try your hand at what it would be like to take your DNA, mix it with your partner's, and discover what kind of interesting new human stew you might create. And from there, if from out of your primordial soup rises a fresh, new, tiny human, you will henceforth learn the art of ultimate sacrifice—what self-lessness truly entails.

I don't think you're ever "ready" to have children. Perhaps, if you wait until your forties, or later, you're more ready than people in their late twenties. But I'll never know. Because by twenty-eight, we decided to take the plunge and throw caution to the wind. We were going to see if we could do it. And by do it, I mean sex. Unprotected. For the children.

Apparently, young people become pregnant, fast. We were both twenty-nine when Ruby Sioux Trohman was born. She was not the curly-haired boy posited by Marie. She was, and still is, a beautiful, smart, funny, straight-haired girl full of heart and empathy who never stops thinking about the world around her. She was originally to be born April 20, 2014, to share her birthday with Adolf Hitler, and on the day when stoners do more of what they do every day, which is get stoned. She ended up arriving four days later. Oh well.

I was, and still am, so glad to have a girl. My brother is a boy. My cousins are boys. My band members are boys. My life is a gay Mötley Crüe song. So I was so excited to be surrounded by some feminine energy. I know that sounds remarkably virtue signally and corny, but it's true. I often get asked, "Don't you want a boy? One you can throw the ball around with? One you can leer with? One you can be a strong, muscular man with?"

As posited throughout this bookish tome, I never played an organized sport in my life. I don't understand football. I don't care about baseball. What shape is a basketball? I don't know! "Do you even gain, bro?" Yeah, weight! I like to sit around. The only sport I play is bowling, a rotund man's game. I do enjoy *Star Wars* and *Lord of the Rings*. Philip K. Dick and Richard Matheson. Kids in the Hall and The State. I collect toys and comics. I almost flunked out of middle school because I was too busy playing *Final Fantasy*. But I'm not a manly man. And my primary interests—while traditionally hoarded by men so afraid of women that many have become avowed men's rights activists—are quite easy to share with a child of any gender construct.

As Ruby has gotten older, we have bonded over everything from *Jaws* to *Back to the Future*. I took her to see *Jurassic World*, and upon watching the *Indominus rex* tear apart an elite squad of dinosaur killers, she exclaimed, "Aw yeah! Raining blood!" She has, of her own accord, fallen so in love with things horror adjacent that she asked for her eighth birthday to be bloodbath themed. I promise, I did not encourage this. But am I proud? Abso-fucking-lutely.

We connect hard, not just over our love for genre but also over the fact that we can have open, honest conversations. We both have the gift of gab, so these discourses tend to be long, drawn-out, and mundane. That's the Trohman way: talk forever about nothing. I find that important, not just for our relationship but for showing Ruby that I care about what she thinks and that I'm always available to talk. I want her to know I am an open book (to an extent that is healthy) and she can trust that I will be forthright with her, never obfuscating my feelings or pushing her away or shutting down, like my mom often did with me.

That destroyed my sense of self-importance. And it took me such a long time, and so much therapy, to find a scintilla of self-esteem. I see myself in Ruby, a truly sensitive child who does need support and validation from her parents to assist in finding that self-confidence. In my mind, she should just be confident in herself because she is so very awesome. But what partly makes her awesome is that she isn't full of herself, no matter how charmed her life is. She is introspective and cares for others. She has awareness of her actions, to a fault at times. She's hard on herself. So it's my job to let her know, on a regular basis, that she's doing great, that she should take it easy on Ruby—I have her back.

So no, I don't wish I had boys. Boys use their fists to get their point across, just as my brother and I did time and time again. I would obviously love a son as much as any other child, but apparently my testicular tadpoles weren't angling for tiny wieners. I love my girls. And yes, I mean girls. Because four years post–Ruby Sioux, Marie gave birth to the second of our tight brood, Zayda Mae, kicker of inflamed balls.

Whereas Ruby came out a never-sleeping baby who grew into a thoughtful, cautious child, Zayda started as the dream baby, always sleeping and smiling. Then the dream child took a hard left, becoming both our homegrown maniac and resident physical comedian. She's the type of kid who likes to stick her fingers in sockets, climb on the unclimbable, and kick her way out of any scenario she finds unsuitable. Zayda knows what she wants and isn't afraid to get it. I love that about her. I was never that confident, never that bold. She's the opposite of both me and her sister, in that regard. She's tougher than I am. She isn't afraid of taking risks or making it very clear when something is not her bag. She's a little tiny baby boss.

But I suppose that's common among most toddlers, a penchant for bossiness. While Ruby maintained a great deal of her personality from toddlerhood on, Zayda may very well *not* stay the way she is. It's hard to know, and I don't want to pigeonhole the lady, not yet. But here's what I know about her as of now: she prefers wearing cheap Disney princess costumes to bed, she's deathly afraid of houseflies and moths, she loves our dog, and she occasionally may yell, "Penis!" out the car window. The fact that she knows the power of a dick joke at age three . . . well, not much could make this idiot any more proud.

Yet behind this child's wonderfully unbridled insanity, there is an incredibly sweet and affectionate girl. Ruby may desire just a short embrace to fill her emotional cup. I respect that. But Zayda, she's like her dad, and her dad's dad before—lots of hugs, lots of kisses, and don't *ever* stop. Never ever. Ever. Is it off-brand for a guy in a rock band to admit that all he's ever wanted is a small daughter to hug and kiss? Perhaps. But in case you didn't read the title of the book, my life has never been about being rock-able.

Having grown up surrounded by so much emotional discomfort, longing for warm connection, I couldn't be more grateful for my snuggly kiddo. And I relish the fact that Zayda wants that as much as I do. I'm so pleased that she's still little enough to be carried. Sometimes I want to squeeze her so hard that her tiny head pops off. And then I'll pick that head up, put it right back on that peanut neck, and kiss it to heck. I don't care. I love that mini-lady.

Do you hate farts? If the answer is yes, then you probably think I'm a bad dad. Because I find it incredibly important to teach my kids the virtue of a solid beefing. And if you think it's truly awful, lowly, and contemptible that I allow my sweet little babes to watch cartoons or expose the older of the two to age-appropriate horror and heavy metal, then lock me up. Put me in jail with all the big baddies on the block: Green River. The BTK. The Happy Face Killer. Why not? You're perfect. And I'm clearly a piece of shit. Give me the chair. I don't give a fuck.

But here's the thing: my kids are smart. They understand that while we can have belching contests and discuss the concept of murder, against the backdrop of Sideshow Bob trying to kill Bart, they know that we don't let body gases out in public, that horror movies are fake, that good manners are incredibly important, and that we always appreciate the things we have. Also, we *don't* murder. That's a big no-no in our household.

As significant as it is that I have fun with my children, it's equally crucial that my wife and I bestow upon them the values of being meaningful and positive societal influences. Kindness and respect are paramount. This is dually important because, by virtue of growing up shepherded by two successful parents, these young ladies are inherently wealthy. They're rich kids. Are they spoiled brats? Mmm, I hope not! We do our best to make sure they are made aware of their social status and know that others are not as fortunate as we are. They're growing up in a city with one of the worst homeless epidemics in the country. They go to school in Los Angeles. They do not live in a bubble, and we intended it that way. Our girls, as sweet and precious as they are, need to be exposed to life and see how people live on the other side. They need to not only garner an appreciation for what they have but gain empathy for those who have not.

Parenting isn't a single-track job. There isn't a straight line with existing points of contact that, if hit correctly, result in excellence. You can do a great job raising your kids, only to end up with children who resent you. You can do a terrible job, be neglectful, and still somehow end up with good kids. Yes, nurture makes a difference, but nature plays such a huge part too. I know my children are getting the nurture. That was in play since before they were born. But the most amazing element of my two wonderful girls is that, inherently, they are naturally wonderful. They were born good.

I have spent two decades building a career in music. I have a band that, at the end of the day, will most likely be etched within the veritable music history books. And yes, I obsess over my work. I obsess so much. Even after volleying from music to attempted television, I continue to obsess. But my career obsessions pale in comparison to my obsession with my kids. Everything I do these days, it's for my girls. I make things and work hard because I want to inspire them to do the same one day. I know they're smarter, funnier, and all-around better than I could ever dream of being. They're really my favorite people in the world. I'm their biggest fan. I want to give them every tool possible so they can grow into whomever they are meant to be. I can't wait to see who they one day become.

As a younger man, I did not imagine my future children. But growing older, I love to imagine my children in the future. Nothing makes me happier.

# Get Back . . . Surgery

I have a shitty back. Technically, it's called a sloppy spine. Medically, it's referred to as degenerative disk disease, which from here out I'll call DDD, but don't confuse that with massive tits. This disease resides in my lower back and means that the disks between the vertebrae are prone to herniating (i.e., slipping). And when these disks decide to take a vacay from their cozy home between the bones, they push against what is known as the sciatic nerve. The nerve pain that ensues isn't so much local to the back as it is a searing, torturous burn that shoots down my leg, normally my right. This makes it impossible to sit, stand, or walk. I'd rather stick a hot butter knife up my penis than feel that feeling ever again.

My DDD was passed down genetically, a gift I have yet to thank my parents for, but I still have a living one left, so there's time! This fabulous disorder has resulted in multiple back surgeries to relieve myself from pain caused by two herniated disks—the first rupture at the ripe age of seventeen and the second at thirty. This procedure is called a partial discectomy, meaning the doctors would cut open my back and remove *only* the part of the disk that was sticking out from my spine, not the entire disk; the healthy portion would stay. It's the misunderstanding of many that this procedure relieves back pain, but it actually relieves horrible sciatic leg pain. That's not to say I had no back pain; I always had back pain. I just learned to tolerate it—it became the normal.

These procedures and pains, and subsequent aging, changed the way I had to perform onstage. As I've previously expounded upon, I used to run around like a dangerous, knife-wielding schizoid—jumping off walls and ten-foot-tall drum risers, landing like a fool with no regard for my spinal column, and spinning around with my guitar like a tornado, a move fans affectionately called "the Trohmania." I was, in a sense, a crucial part of Fall Out Boy's earlier visual production for many years. But I had to stop doing all that once I became a Mick Mars, of sorts: a stage statue.

When I stopped my antics, I believe a lot of fans thought I was angry at the band or at the fans themselves. I was angry, sure . . . but about my back. Sure, I was probably mad at my band too, but only in the way that brothers get mad at one another for simply existing too much, and too often, within one another's physical space. No, most of my anger was due to chronic, severe spine, nerve, and muscle pain. Most people enjoy their youth without much awareness of the importance of their skeletal, nervous, and muscular systems. Conversely, I spent my youth with so much awareness that I envied people who could perform mind-blowing tasks such as standing up straight, walking without a limp, and enjoying a good, long sit without the prospect of creeping searing lumbar and leg pain. For many years, this was my state of being, along with the prospect that, eventually, I would likely endure future back surgeries to correct eventual disk issues.

Around thirty-four, I received a stem cell injection to prevent a third disk herniation. The American health care system is a toxic waste dump, so those procedures are not covered by insurance. Stem cells save lives, and I guess insurance companies don't like the idea of healthy people they can't invoice. So I paid out of pocket. Despite the expense, I was happy with the procedure because it worked well, for about three years. I felt great. I started moving a little more onstage—never like in my twenties, but still, I could "rock outward" a little. I also started to weight train. I got stronger. I felt like what I assumed a normal human being feels like until middle age hits: somewhat invincible.

Then, at thirty-seven, my back gave out again. This was during the height of the COVID-19 pandemic. I was still strength training, outdoors, masked (don't you worry!) under the guidance of a personal instructor (don't you worry, twice!). Despite the precautions, and the stem cells, I thought I had screwed the pooch, lifted too heavy, and herniated another disk. Just when I stupidly thought I had beaten my own chronic illness, it turns out it was always there, waiting in the shadows, lurking around the corner.

But this pain, it was different. I know what a herniation feels like; it comes with that nearly instantaneous, torturous shooting leg pain. This wasn't that. This pain *was* local to my back. It felt deep and hollow, as if something had collapsed. I thought, whatever this was, it was caused by lifting too much, and I felt like a real pumpkin head who should have known better. Yet it turned out that, in fact, the weight training had *saved* my spine from falling apart sooner.

Upon review of an MRI, it was discovered that one of my older disks had nearly vanished. *Poof.* Disappeared. I wasn't herniated this time. This disk, it was just done. And what was left behind was nearly bone on bone—vertebrae grinding into each other. I could feel it every time I got up from a sitting position or bent down to pick up a sock. I started to feel for our pepper mill.

Initially, the pain was horrid. Then it went away. Soon after that, it became an intermittent issue: sometimes I'd be laid out; other times I'd feel totally fine. I continued to consult my spine doctor and discuss options for future treatment. Along the way, I tried several epidural cortisone shots, all to varying degrees of effect. Some gave me relief. Some made me sick to my stomach. Some did nothing. There's a limit to how many shots you can take before enough is medically enough. I hit that limit.

After that, the pain became severe and constant. Around late November to early December 2021, the situation turned into an emergency; I had to act. I received a second MRI, which showed that things had degraded much further over the past three months. From there, my options became clear: I had to get a new disk put in my spine—a procedure simply referred to as disk replacement surgery.

While the approach to the partial discectomies was made local to the area of herniation (i.e., the back) and the procedures were relatively easy to recover from, this one would be different—far more invasive. It involved going through my abdomen this time, which meant cutting through my stomach muscles, then moving and/or removing organs to get to my spine. And that section of one's spinal region, the L4/L5 area, is very vascular, meaning that there are many fragile blood vessels in the way. This meant that, along with a spine surgeon, a vascular surgeon would need to be present, as the likelihood of nicking vessels and losing blood was high. And as it turns out, I lost blood. A *lot*. So once the doctors got done putzing around in there and stopping the blood loss, *then* they took what amounted to a spinal car jack and cranked open my spine so they could bore a metal disk into my vertebrae—one that can't slip and slide anywhere. Then the organs plop back in, the stomach gets slapped back together, and voilà. Easy peasy!

I had the procedure on December 27, 2021: a Christmas gift to myself. As a Jewish kid, I always had a reverence for Christmas—a much more bright and exciting winter holiday than the one with the eight-point-five candles on a menorah. I had my surgery done at a private hospital in Orange County, where I was allowed to spend one day recovering before I spent the rest of my recovery time at home in my own bed. I had been informed, time and time again, by the surgeons, the nurses, my wife, and the papers they sent me home with, that this was a *major* surgery. And thus, everyone made it clear that I needed to do nothing but rest—no work, no stress. Yet due to the fact that I thought I knew best, since I'd had experiences with prior back surgeries, coupled with the fact that I was as high as the Burj Khalifa in Dubai on narcotic painkillers, I continued working through the post-op, meaning I kept going *while* recovering *and* withdrawing from narcotics. Mistake.

Many would classify the way I handled this as poorly. Others would really delve into the issues and say that I was awfully foolish to presume that I could work on editing a television pilot presentation while I was recovering from major spine surgery and withdrawing from pill-form heroin. Tomato, other pronunciation of tomato. The point is, due to working and stressing, the two things I was specifically told not to do, throughout the initial portion of my post-op, I had a legit mental breakdown in January 2022. This is not hyperbole— one day I went catatonic for twelve hours. I was in a full-on dissociative state; my body had said, "No more!" I went into protective mode. I had had enough.

My depression, my anxiety, it had taken over to the max. I became the most suicidal I had been since I was a teenager, and I was beyond irrational. I was having obsessive thoughts about work that were harmful to myself and those around me. It also came to light that I had been in a compulsive mode of working since that past June. I liken this long journey into madness to rappelling down a deep, dark cavern, one that has no bottom as far as I know. And as I continued down that hole, I eventually reached a blackness devoid of any light. That is when I broke.

I had left myself no space for healing, either physically or mentally. What compounds the awful nature of the situation is that my state scared the living daylights out of my wife and oldest daughter—the former concerned about needing to 5150 me, the latter just worried about Daddy. I was not in control of myself. At least, not totally. Luckily, with help from my wife, I procured a modicum of awareness and was reminded of the support system I had in place for my mental health.

I made a call to my psychiatrist. I broke down in tears. She never admonished me, but she did let me know that we had gone too long without checking in with each other. She made it clear that this couldn't happen again and told me how much she cared, which made me cry more. I'm not a "man's man," and I have no problem with crying; I'm just not very good at it. So whatever well of tears had been building up behind the dam, it came bursting out. It felt good to cry.

My doctor—we'll call her Dr. Sanders—promptly changed my medication to a cocktail that I can safely say has saved me, or at least led me toward a path of calm. Whatever your opinions about medication for the brain are, I do not care to hear them. I can only speak for me. I know I am unbalanced, chemically speaking, and that I need to be on at least one, if not multiple, medications to maintain balance.

Dr. Sanders also gave me strict orders to stop working, orders that I wish I had listened to the first time around. But here's the thing: I'm bad at not working. Not only does my job entail creating, and creating is my *favorite* thing to do, but I *might* also be a workaholic. Despite my inability to stay totally addicted to any substance for long enough periods of time to be considered a boozehound, coke whore, dope fiend, needler, angel dust buster, crackhead, guy with meth breath, green leaf goon, or just a plain old cigarillo smith, work is something I can't kick so easily. Yet I was working on a completely unhealthy level, with more projects than one human can hold upon their Atlas shoulders—I was making multiple comics, developing several television projects, writing this book (yeah, this one), writing scripts, and attempting to make a record. So I had to off-load. And going backward on my list, I started with the most important of my jobs: my FOBusiness.

As of late 2021, Fall Out Boy began to work on new music. It's hard to predict whether, by the time you're reading this, these songs will have turned into an album or whether that album has even been announced. I hope it has either been released or shelved, because I do not want to ruin the surprise, upend the mystery, reveal where the Waldo is, etc.

For the first time in years, I actually love where Fall Out Boy is going with these songs—if this becomes an album, it will surely be a guitar album. Not only does that speak to me, the *guitarist* in the band, but I have been more a part of the process from the ground up than I have been in years. I feel a personal connection to these songs.

That's partly why it was so hard for me to call Patrick and tell him what was going on, that my recovery from surgery had gone poorly, that I had gone cuckoo for Cocoa Puffs, and that both my spine and brain doctors had ordered me to stop work, in an effort to keep me from dying—not being dramatic, just relaying reality. I had to keep in mind that Patrick is my friend first and he cares about me. Deep down, I knew he was going to be supportive. Yet I was nervous that the collective band, and our management, would keep chugging along without me.

The way Fall Out Boy used to work was as follows: Pete wrote lyrics in a book, of sorts. Patrick got those lyrics, put them to music, and thus came the songs you love. I'm simplifying the process, but that's the gist. Yes, here and there I would inject a tune, but that was not how things would normally begin. I am not the switch, just part of the contraption. Once there was a song, or several songs, from those guys that excited the collective band, and management, then the recording process would start. And once that process started, there was no stopping it. It was all about the machine and less about the individuals who make it.

I do not mean this pejoratively. When you are in a massive group, one that has reached a level beyond your peers, a status as a pop culture entity, there's this need, or at least a desire, to stay relevant. Relevance is sustenance, and sustenance is life. So if we lose relevance, we lose life. And we, the band, cannot stay relevant without music. New music, to be exact. Otherwise, we could be relegated to an emo mummy of yesteryear, a dusty early-2000s relic.

Although we've made albums that might have turned some of you off, me included sometimes, the reasons we experimented with cowriting, samples, less guitar-driven and more synth-driven music were to push the boundaries of the band

and find a relevant place within the current music landscape. That landscape, if you haven't noticed, *hates* guitars. Thus, finding that balance where we could get guitars to exist on pop radio has been a struggle, to say the least.

If we made *From Under the Cork Tree* eight times in a row, we'd be servicing a small percentage of people who cannot move on, which would be depressing. Thankfully, most people do move on. That is life, whether you like it or not. One can argue, and I have many times, that the ways that we moved were perhaps not true to what a band should sound like, but that's subjective, and I am only a quarter of the voice that is Fall Out Boy. I also like a lot of the "poppier" stuff we made from 2013 through 2015. It's not all black-and-white, even when it comes down to my own feelings.

So back to the way the machine used to work. If someone were to, let's say, "thwart" the process, it was likely that that person would get steamrolled out of the way. During *Infinity on High*, no one was concerned I was only half there, mostly on hard drugs. It's not that there wasn't love in the air; we were just overtaken by the sheer force of the massive apparatus moving forward in a way that was working—songs were hits, money was rolling in, and arenas were selling out. Why knock it?

With latter records, like *Save Rock & Roll* and *American Beauty/American Psycho*, I had expressed my reservations about the less acoustic approach (i.e., the band not sounding like two guitars, a bass, and drums up front and center). I'm sure I expressed these reservations in a sideways, blunt, and not so careful manner. But even if I hadn't, and I cannot recollect for certain, my input wouldn't have changed our trajectory. The machine was moving, it was working, and nothing would stop it. Again, why fix what doesn't seem to be broken?

Cut to 2022, and we're working on these new songs. I had this major surgery, this mental breakdown. Then my dog of eleven years, my best friend, my little potato French bulldog, Louie, had a sudden stroke and died. For those of you with dogs, you most likely understand my profound grief. In many ways, losing Louie, who I had cupped in my hands as a baby and raised through his senior years, had been worse than losing a mother who, at many junctures, had cared far less for me. For those of you who think I should just get over it, you probably don't like dogs and maybe have hurt or murdered dogs, you fucking psychopaths.

Outside of my devastation and mourning, I had all of this physical and mental pain I was managing. I was trying to get my raging depression and anxiety under control with these brand-new medications. I was a mess, to say the least, and my life felt like a never-ending dumpster fire, to say the most. With all of that in play, which is more legitimately serious than disliking a sound or a direction the band is going in, I was still most concerned that if I expressed that I could not handle working on these new songs, I would be excused from the process.

This frightened me greatly because for the first time in many years, I was so thrilled to be making a Fall Out Boy album again—the guitar-heavier album I had been fighting for us to make for almost a decade. With these songs, I was very involved from the ground up, and I didn't want to lose my place in line. I was scared that if I needed time away to heal, the old ways of the band would come into play and the machine would run me over.

While I may be one of the better communicators in the band, I was afraid to confront this situation. I needed to find calm and comfort somewhere, something to bring me down from my tower of anxiety and give me some confidence before we had these conversations. And then, as if divine intervention were a real thing, my old friend Gordon Ball came over to check on me. In the midst of trading sad-boy stories, our favorite depressive pastime, he asked if I had watched the Beatles' *Get Back* docuseries, three "episodes" (i.e., two-plus-hour movies) directed by Peter Jackson.

I respect the Beatles; everyone should. As a collective, they made about twenty-one albums' worth of nearly perfectly crafted songs over the course of just eight years. I'm not a huge Beatles guy, but that is fucking impressive. There's always the question, "Who's better, the Beatles or the Stones?" The Stones have been around for about sixty years. They have made thirty albums. Of those thirty albums, maybe five songs have an identity. The rest sound the same to me. I am sorry; disagree all you want, and please, love the Stones and hate me. But I am speaking my truth. I actually love those five songs, by the way. The other four thousand white-guy-blues standards? Nerp.

The reason I am coming to this perhaps wild conclusion is to further cement that even though I am not a big Beatles guy, I have immense respect for them and their songwriting career. So when Gordon asked me if I had seen *Get Back*, I said, "No. Why should I?"

Gordon replied, "Man, watching George Harrison interact with the rest of the band *really* reminded me of you."

That sold me, not because I like me or I like to fantasize that I'm George Harrison, but because I was in this perfect place in my life to watch something that might make me feel less alone about feeling alone in Fall Out Boy. So the next day I put on *Get Back*. Now, first off, watching these guys rehearse, for the first time ever, "Let It Be" and "I Me Mine" or witnessing Paul write the titular track from scratch is a religious experience. You don't have to be a Beatles nut to go crazy for these behind-the-curtain looks at how the sausage is made.

But when we get to the moments where George becomes frustrated with his bandmates, when he tells Paul, "I'll play, you know, whatever you want me to play, or I won't play at all if you don't want me to play. Whatever it is that will please you, I'll do it." I literally told the same thing to my band over the pandemic, via video chat, when we were discussing the state of the band and a potential follow-up to *Mania*.

I had such a crummy time with that album. What many people do not know is I had written a grip of songs that almost made the record but were trashed at the top of that recording process, which pushed me over the edge, and I refused to take part in the rest of that record. I regret that only because I do not love the outcome, and perhaps if I had stayed involved, I could have sprayed some of my creative juices into the mix, thus altering the substance and making my selfish being slightly happier. However, knowing what place we were all in at the time, that is probably some unlikely wishful thinking. Plus, time travel—not so real.

So during that video chat, I said I did not want to write a lot of songs yet again, only to have one or two make it on the album. I wanted to be told what was wanted of me and how it was wanted; if you want my music, tell me. If you don't, no problem. If you want me to just play guitar and shut up, I'm happy to do it, and if you want me to fuck off and just show up to live gigs, I'll do that too. Just tell me!

When George attempted to submit his now iconic song "All Things Must Pass" and was denied, you not only got a window into how this talented guy was boxed out of his own band but how he was also an island unto himself. I had similar experiences of submitting what I thought were my best tracks, only to have them ignored. It happens; that's part of the process. And I would take those songs and craft them to work for other projects, often The Damned Things. But that still didn't remove the hurt that went along with being rejected by those I wanted to impress the most.

It's made clear that Harrison was this solo writer working against the all-powerful Lennon/McCartney partnership. In a way, that has always been me alongside Patrick and Pete. It's no wonder why Harrison became fed up and quit midrehearsal for what would ultimately become *Let It Be*. He was pushed.

Watching this all happen in "real time" made me feel less alone about being in a dysfunctionally functional band for two decades. Yeah, I guess I'm saying I'm the George Harrison of Fall Out Boy, a much shittier George Harrison, but that's the closest analog I have found. But also, watching Lennon, McCartney, and Starr try again and again to get their friend back into the fold reminded me of something I had forgotten: My band loves me. And I them.

There was never any malice. One could say, "It's just business, baby!" But that's not how the guys approach Fall Out Boy. It truly is a creative endeavor, and that comes with awareness blinders. I remember speaking with Clay Tarver, who was in the seminal NYC noise band Chavez and is now a successful writer and director. He perfectly explained that being in a band is like forming an unholy trinity. But he was in a threepiece. "Quadrinity" doesn't have as nice a ring to it. Regardless, he's not wrong. We are a band of very different people, with incredibly different points of view that often clash. What brought us together, in part, is the simple fact that we all wanted to be in a band. But we also wanted to be in a band with each other, because at the end of the day, we are friends. And no one else wanted to do it with us.

I called Patrick a couple of days after finishing *Get Back*. I told him what had happened to me, and he immediately said that my health is more important than a bunch of songs. I almost cried. Patrick then put an instant four-week hold on working on these songs any further so I could get back on my feet.

As of this writing, I am able to walk again.

# Finally, the End!

I never wanted to write a book. Well, at least I had never planned to write a book. And definitely not a book about me. I don't like me. I think I've made that perfectly clear. I surely don't like me enough to write about me just for the hell of it. But I suppose I don't know what I would write about otherwise. I mean, no one's begging for a psychosexual spy thriller straight from the guy most known for not being known for being in Fall Out Boy. And most of the time, when people find out I'm in the band, they (a) are awestruck and (b) ask me, "When did you join the band?" So that prompts the question "Who would want to read *any* book written by me?" Since you're reading this, *you* know the answer. And I really should be thanking you. That's me thanking you.

It was my lit manager, Ari, who proposed the idea that a book about my life would be an interesting read. And much like when I incessantly begged my father to buy me a guitar, wearing him down to a pulp, Ari had unceasingly pressured me on the idea that I write a book. And so, beaten into malleable submission like tender vittles, I did it—mostly so Ari would stop asking me to write a book.

But I do like to write, despite my weak protests. I might like writing words more than playing the guitar. And as evidenced by the thousands of words I wrote professing my love of the guitar, I hope you take me at my word regarding my feelings about words. Writing is something that has always come to me a little more naturally than music. Yet I can't help but shake the feeling that it's an incredibly cocky move to write a memoir, of sorts, before hitting a respectable memoir age of, say, midfifties and beyond.

Trying to hock this memoir is only slightly cockier than when, in my early twenties, I had the balls to harshly shut down a member of Def Leppard. It was the early 2000s, the "golden era" of emo, and Fall Out Boy was playing a pretaped awards show for VH1 called *Big in '05*. I was wearing an Iron Maiden shirt that day. I don't remember if we had just played or if we were about to hit the stage, but I was incredibly stoned and *very* paranoid. So my plan for the remainder of the event was to have as few interactions as humanly possible. Thus, I created an invisible barrier of safety around me. All I had to do was not let any unknowns penetrate that barrier, which was made up and thus not real. But hey, weed.

As I paced back and forth in front of the door to our dressing room, lost in my own head, unaware of the outside world, Rick Savage, the bassist of Def Leppard, approached me. He looked at me, and I froze. Rick didn't introduce himself; he only looked down to the image of Eddie on my shirt and said, with facetious, British candor, "Where's your Def Leppard shirt? In the wash?" Despite how high I was, which was very, or how nervous this was making me, which was very, I managed to look Rick straight in the eye and reply, cold as ice, "No." Then, as I continued to stare through him, he walked off, bewildered and, it seemed to me at the time, crestfallen. Then *I* proceeded to feel like an asshole.

I have mentioned the phenomenon of time slowing down in a potentially deadly experience. Well, in the moment when Rick approached me, time became as thick and runny as molasses. Like I was moments before the van wreck that nearly killed us all, I was again in panic mode. It'd be fair to say that because I was only twenty-one at the time, I wasn't making wise decisions, such as considering that _maybe_ smoking a thumb-sized blunt before appearing on a nationally televised awards show would not result in a reasonable, enjoyable experience.

From the outside, it felt like I had big-timed a big-timer. I like Def Leppard a lot. _Pyromania_ is such an incredible album, perfectly uniting stadium rock, massive pop hooks, and sonic production that still kills today. And I like Rick Savage. I don't know why I said what I said. It sucked. I mean, sure, what he said was sort of a bad joke. But I didn't have to be such a prick about it. I suppose I was protecting myself from exposure as a vulnerable young man, even more fragile due to the overindulgence of the green leaf. Maybe, within my lingering subconscious, there was a need to volley back, a pseudo-punk "fuck the establishment" mentality. Perhaps I was also mirroring how I had seen my acerbic mother deal with people in the wild; her vitriolic ways of interacting had earned her very few, if any, allies in her sixty-two years.

In 2017, Fall Out Boy would play Rock in Rio literally right under Def Leppard, who played under Aerosmith. We hung out with guitarist Phil Collen. He's in his sixties and _incredibly_ ripped. I'm in my thirties and have the incredibly soft, sweet physique of a Pillsbury cookie dough roll. So that didn't feel great, seeing how hard I don't try. But it's not his fault that he does reps or eats clean. Good for him. Phil's a cool guy. I was nervous I'd run into his bandmate, Rick, and that he would remember our interaction. That didn't happen. I then got to play in front of at least one hundred thousand rabid Brazilians. The show went well. I didn't mess up. And I got to tell people I played with Aerosmith and Def Leppard. But Aerosmith probably doesn't know that.

I'm lucky. Not just because of the success. But I get to be in a massive band while staying relatively incognito. I can go *anywhere* in the world and not a rat's rear is given regarding my presence. Outside of diehard fans of my band, no one knows who the hell I am. And I've never been so happy to not be cared about.

For instance, when Fall Out Boy travels through an airport and people recognize the other guys, these people often ask for photos. And nine out of ten times, that fan will ask *me* to take the photo. It's great. Really, I love going with the bit, pretending that I work for the guys. It only gets awkward when the person asking for the photo realizes I am in the band *after* the pic has been taken. That person then profusely apologizes, as if I'm the one hurting, and proceeds to ask for a second photo, as if to soothe my wounded ego. That's the moment when I inform them of the bad news, that their camera is out of film. They then tell me it's a cell phone. I shrug. Awkward silence ensues as I walk off to board some plane to somewhere. We will never meet again.

When I was younger, I had virtually no confidence. So interactions such as those *really* bothered me. They would make me feel invisible, undesirable, unimportant. To be seen, or not be seen, as an important cog in Fall Out Boy's infrastructure by every Tom, Dickless, and Harry Balls used to chip away at my fragile psyche. Instead of resting secure in the knowledge that I was very much in this band—a band I had started—I relied on validation from complete strangers to feel like a real boy. What a sad way of being.

I used to think I wanted that facial recognition. But what would it have afforded me? Rogue disturbances from unknowns around every corner? And what would the purpose of that fame be? I understand the logistical purpose of fortune—to have lots of money, to buy lots of things. I like things. Things make sense. And sure, fame is sometimes a by-product of fortune. But we're living in an age when people are genuinely concerned with fame, first and foremost. I don't understand that. I know I've felt the same pull at times, but I don't care for it. I prefer unmitigated space to do my own thing, unhindered.

In retrospect, I never really wanted the fame I thought I wanted. And I never aspired to have a fortune of any sort. I've done well, financially, but it's no fortune. Jeff Bezos has a fortune. But he doesn't have hair. I have hair. Lots of hair. And if hair were money, I'd be a plutocrat. I'm covered in rich, plentiful tufts. My beard grows up to my eyes. My legs are encased in bear pants. My eyebrows have a healthy relationship with one another. My ears wear mittens. I have built-in shoulder pads. Hobbit feet. Fuzzy knuckles. Nostril coifs. Back bristles. Knee sprouts.

I'm engulfed in my own hair. And so by all accounts, it's crystal clear who is richer. It's Jeff Bezos. He's way richer. But I'm still in a more advantageous monetary position than most. I won't deny it. I'm a wealthy, straight white Jewish man who's damn lucky to be able to partake in the spoils from his big band while maintaining complete anonymity.

I am more than contented as the guitarist, the guy behind the guys, the occasional writer, the father, the husband, and the proud owner of a chunky, bottom-burping dog. I'm OK with being onstage, but I don't want the spotlight on me. I love playing guitar, but I don't need to solo. OK, fine, I will occasionally solo. I want to be with funny people and write jokes, but I don't need to be the star—the funniest person in the room. I'm best when I am a part of the mix and helping to keep the train on the tracks. Whether I'm the "glue guy" in Fall Out Boy, the person who kicks off a writing project enough so it can get traction, the spouse who helps pick up around the house, or the dad who rushes the screaming kid into the other room to save everyone else the trouble, I'm here for it.

My family recently got a new pup. His name is Gary. He's now a ten-month-old English bulldog who weighs nearly sixty-five pounds. He smells like fish and sleeps with his tongue half out of his mouth. My eldest dog, often referred to as my firstborn son, the late Louie, lived to be an eleven-year-old French bulldog. He was half of Gary's size. Louie hated Gary.

When Gary arrived in our home, he and Louie were about the same size. And as puppies do, Gary would annoy Lou. So, in turn, Louie would show Gary who was boss by pinning the Gar-bear to the ground and humping him into shameful submission. But then Gary grew. A lot. Within a week, he became twice the size of Louie. Then he could not be fucked into submission. Gary had transformed from a pile of wet towels to an immovable wall of grade-A beef. He is a powerful meat barrier who taunted Louie on a regular basis with his size and strength. Gary's an adorable, enchanting, round, stinky jerk. Poor, poor Louie. The question then has to be asked: Who's humping who now?

Last week, Gary broke into my wife's office and ate a bunch of fabric samples. What an asshole. He's a Hoover. I pulled a battery from his mouth earlier today. Louie was never that way. I bought Louie when I was hungover, after a night of hard drinking, on a whim. Outside of his separation anxiety, he was a calm canine. And he never chewed up our stuff.

Gary was planned. We thought hard about getting him. He was intended to be the dog we knew we'd need once Louie ascended to the great dog bed in the sky. So after Gary ate all that chemically tempered fabric, he ran through the backyard and into our dining room to perform a well-coordinated fecal spray into our home's air-return vent. His aim was true; the shit went far into the ducts. And without the proper tools, or eight-foot-long arms, we were forced to hire a professional vent-cleaning service to professionally clean dog shit from the ducts so we wouldn't have to inhale bits of dog diarrhea into our lungs night and day.

I did not know there was a company that existed to clean air vents. I guess vents need love too. That's logical and boring. But as a person who has spent most of his past twenty-two years on earth touring the world, unable to participate in domestic life, I find the mundane exciting. I like to sweep, wipe, fold, stack, organize, *and* scrub. And now, after all this time living as a nomad, I yearn to be at home, to clean my way into the abyss. I like to think that my touring for decades has earned me the right to enjoy my home, to be with my family, and to discover more guys for more things, like the ones who use a long suction tube to suck puppy shit from the guts of a house.

There's a certain comfort in being on the road. In some ways, it's my second nature. When I show up to the start of a tour, I instantly fall into my place, into old routines. But while I thoroughly enjoy the live-music element, once the show is over, the remainder of touring circumstances make for a strange way to live. My day-to-day schedule becomes very amorphous, driven only by a requirement to do an hour or two of work every other day. Otherwise, I am left to my own devices. So it's incredibly easy to fall into a routine of "no routine," rife with pot smoke, endless movie watching, video games out the wazoo, or just idly staring at the wall, daydreaming about wishing I had something fulfilling to do.

In my twenties, I enjoyed much of this transient, structureless lifestyle. My twenties had very little structure to begin with, and I wasn't as desperate to plant roots. I wasn't married yet; I didn't have kids. I had youthful exuberance and figured that I had found my calling, my career, the end of the line—and a good one at that. It was a career that allowed me to fuck off nearly all day. And fucking off all day is a correct way to proceed when you're in your twenties.

But I'm nearly forty now. I don't like to fuck off anymore. My depression worsens when I don't have a schedule to adhere to. If I wake up past eight in the morning, I panic, worried I have wasted my entire day. The specter of death, while hopefully far off, feels more palpable. I don't want to waste my waning days stoned, lost in B horror films and half-baked first-person shooters. I want to be in my children's lives. I want to hug my wife, every day. I want to enjoy the spoils of my victories that I've worked so hard to afford. And I'm tired. So very tired.

Those of us in the touring world tend to tack additional phantom years onto our own lives, to account for the exhaustion accrued from life on the road. But I'm not old, not technically speaking, on the page. I'm aware that I'm on the tail end of a sort of youth, teetering in my late thirties, fighting the oncoming tide of middle age.

Fall Out Boy toured with Paramore in 2014, the same year my wife gave birth to our firstborn, Ruby. Prior to the tour, and the baby, we had just made the arduous move from New York to Los Angeles. And upon leaving for that tour, I not only left my new family behind but felt as if I had abandoned them.

I had a hard time enjoying what was truly a fantastic run. Sure, I liked the people we were traveling with, and the shows—all at amphitheaters—were incredible. Yet I was heartbroken to be away from my wife and new child. So to attempt to mitigate that, I flew home between dates, which only added immense fatigue and pressure to an already laborious and complex situation. Years later, Marie and I look back at that decision, flabbergasted. It was stupid. I shouldn't have put myself through that ordeal.

I never did a thing like that again. Following that tour, as my family suffered my absence, I became more withdrawn on the road, stuck in a cycle of loneliness. And so when people would see me onstage, despondent, they probably made all kinds of assumptions. But it was because of heartache.

In 2019, a journalist, of sorts, was reviewing Fall Out Boy in Philadelphia. And while moping about during a set, not giving it the all I should have, I was singled out by this critic, who wrote that I had "all the charisma of a Walgreens cashier." I suppose the guy didn't want to go with the old "wet blanket" cliché. I get it, gotta stay ahead of the creative writing curve. But Walgreens? What did they ever do to him? I find the place to be fine. It has all the wares I desire. And I recently had a very nice interaction with a very friendly Walgreens cashier in Washington, DC. She called me sweetie. It was endearing. So why not pick on people more famously apathetic? DMV employees. TSA agents. Gravediggers. "He had all the charisma of a methanol-huffing mortuary assistant." But I'm not the creative writer here. Let the pros do their jobs.

That journalist had caught me on a bad day, in a bad week, in a bad month. I missed my kids. By that point in my life, my second daughter, Zayda, had been pushed forth into existence. And touring, while a privileged way to earn a living, had become a sort of death sentence for me. I wanted to be a father and was concerned my children wouldn't get to know me, and I them.

I tend to get dire. Those kids were going to know me well; I wouldn't have let it go any other way. Touring has not hindered our ability to become thick as thieves. And since my time as the frumpy convenience store attendant, I've had plenty of moments to bond with my kids, plant my roots further, refresh, and reenergize.

Not that living through a global pandemic has been fun for anyone, and I feel like a rotten asshole for writing this, but being forced to quarantine wasn't all bad. It allowed me, a longtime nomad, to enjoy my home for the first time in many years. I finally got to spend time with my family and forge a secondary life in Southern California that has allowed me the freedom to explore different elements of my persona, outside of Fall Out Boy. And with that time afforded, I've been able to break from the band, only to come back to it stronger.

As of this writing, it's been nearly a year since Fall Out Boy completed our first-ever stadium tour. To say it was a religious experience would be wrong, because I never had this much fun in synagogue. It was truly transcendent to come back to live music at a time when everyone needed it more than ever, myself included.

I may have had my ups and downs with the band; I've had my grievances with how things have worked, or not worked. I've complained about perceptions. I've disagreed about the creative. I was a black cloud for a time. And then I stopped. I grew older and became too tired to complain. The past thirty-seven years of my life are gone; they went in an instant. And I don't want to spend the next however many years as fractious as I had been in my youth. Instead of spraying bile upon my bandmates, I want to spray love juice. Metaphorical love juice.

I'm beyond obliged to be alive and thrilled to be doing what I love for a living. And I'm lucky to be able to provide for my family. I do it by swiping at the six strings on my guitar like a slap-happy, anthropomorphized chimpanzee.

So this is the end of my book, I think. You may check to see if there are any hidden, folded pages henceforth. But to my knowledge, this is all I wrote. How was the experience, for you? One to ten? Feel free to fill in your answers on the mail-in review card tucked inside the dust jacket. Go look. I'm not kidding.

Psych!

You stupid butthole! JK! I think you're a really smart butthole. And seriously, thanks for reading. And for forking over the cash or credit or . . . cryptocurrency? Probably not that. I hope the publisher makes their money back. I'd like to write another book. A psychosexual spy thriller. *The Porn Identity? Cunt for the Red Cocktober? The Day of the Jackoff? Thunderballs? The Spy Who Came In from the Cold to Have Hot Sex, and Also Came?* I dunno. You tell me.

# Acknowledgments

I'll try my best to acknowledge those acknowledgeable in chronological order but will ultimately fail—so let's get this fiasco started. First, I must thank my two literary managers, Ari Lubet and Richard Abate, for helping to birth this book. That's how incompetent I am—it takes two managers to get me to write. Without Ari, I most likely would have never written this here treatise. Without Richard, no one would have wanted to make it. So it is to you both I owe eternal thanks. *Especially* if these pages change my life for the better. And if it's for the worse . . . "Thanks!"

Continuing on the theme of thanks, I'd like to bestow much of that to my fabulous editor, Brant Rumble, with whom I spent loads of time intimately working on this book. He doesn't just have an impressive action star name; he's also an impressive human, a real *star* that takes swift *action* when it comes to editing. Did that land? Well, here's what I'm trying to say: it is easy to get lost in the forest when writing two-hundred some odd pages about yourself, and Brant helped me see clearly every step along the way, championing each word I jotted down, doubly so when I doubted myself most. Stephen King famously said, "To write is human, to edit is divine." So here's to Brant and his godlike editorial powers. I bend the knee to thee.

You think I'd forget my band, the Fall Out Boys, but I absolutely never will not, *not* do that. I owe them a *massive* amount of gratitude. When I informed the guys I was writing a book about myself, which inherently would include the band, I imagined the worry that went through their minds: "Will he write about us?" "What kind of horseshit *will* he conjure up?" "What a fucking asshole, using us to sell a book!" Well, they never said that. In fact, they were quite supportive. When I texted them a PDF copy of an early manuscript, I got three thumbs-up emojis in response. That's high praise in 2022. I truly appreciate their trust in me.

Obviously, my amazing wife, Marie Trohman, and my wonderful children, Ruby and Zayda, are owed many *todas*, *dankes*, *mercis*, and other words that mean thanks that we as Americans may not fully understand yet. One day, hopefully. I *believe* in us. Not really. Anyway . . . *gracias, mi familia*! It's the least I can say. They had to be around me, a ball of unbridled stress and anxiety, while I desperately tried to make deadlines. Like the good provider I am, I likely gave each a healthy smattering of PTSD while writing of this book. There were times when I isolated myself from them for days so I could crank out pages. All in all, it wasn't fun to be around me during the process. Yet they understood and expressed pride in what I have since accomplished. I owe them more than anyone for their consistent, loving support. I'm beyond lucky to have them by my side.

My dad has always been a big fan of me and what I do. I can't express the unyielding love and grace I have for this man. I hope he finds this book to be acceptable; I know there are instances in here that were likely hard for him to read. Yet he gave me the space to express how I feel, unadulterated. As well, I give gratitude to my brother, Sam, for the same space and support. Outside of the family I have created, these two are all I have left, and my adoration for them goes beyond the pale.

I have a bevy of people who have influenced and supported every facet of my creative life. Brandon Dermer, without you, I would have never trusted myself to explore the idea of sharing my writing. Spencer Berman, you have read every stupid word I've written and helped make me a half-decent (if that) writer. Outside of fifteen years of friendship, Brian Posehn, we quarantined together for the last two years during the pandemic, writing jokes and making comics. You have championed my craft and made me better and, hopefully, funnier. Rick Remender, you've taken me under your wing and trusted in me, believing I have something to say that's worth putting to paper. Bob McLynn, Jonathan Daniel, Dustin Addis, and all of Crush Management, you have known me since I was a child and helped rear my career. I'm so very fortunate to have you all. Brendan Walter, I am grateful for our honest friendship and adore working together. You *also* read my crap and helped make it *less* crappy. Chris Waters, I cherish our friendship. We have an incredible working relationship that I hope lasts a lifetime. Adam Londy, thank you for your early support and for seeing me as more than just "some guy" from an emo band. And of course, I can't forget my best bud from back in Chicago, Drew Brown. We cut our teeth together. And through thick and thin, we've stayed thick as thieves. You should've been mentioned earlier in this book. I fucked up. Oh well!

The truth is I have so many more people to thank and, as the header indicates, acknowledge: Scott Ian, Isaac Galatzer-Levy, Skylar Pittman, Jeny Quine, Jackson Stewart, Dan Andriano, Keith Buckley, Josh Newton, Steve Kane, Jim Grimes, Mani Mostofi, Bita Mostofi, Neeraj Kane, Gordon Ball—I could go on and on. I have likely forgotten many more wonderful folks who have made me who I am today. I promise I'll carry so much guilt that I'll write another book just to acknowledge you.

That being said, a final grand a'thank-you to the fine folks at Hachette Books for making this book a physical reality. I hope I didn't let you down. And if I did . . . whoops!